Betty Crocker's
KITCHEN
GARDENS

by MARY MASON CAMPBELL

pictures by TASHA TUDOR

GOLDEN PRESS · NEW YORK
Western Publishing Company, Inc.
Racine, Wisconsin

THANK YOU

from the author who extends her grateful
appreciation to those who have given
valuable help and encouragement in the
research and writing of this book.

Contents

iii

Dear Friend,

"To the gardener who loves to cook and the cook who loves to garden," we dedicate this special book on garden lore.

It is a book for the beginner who has never turned a spade or watched a seedling sprout. It is a book for the experienced gardener whose "green thumb" is itching to try an exciting new project. It is for the lover of herbs who has no more space than a sunny windowsill . . . or a salad lover with only a small patch of ground beside the kitchen door. It is for everyone, caught up in this fast-paced world, who will take pleasure in growing something fresh and fragrant and flavorful to enjoy, just moments from picking, at the family table. Or, by preserving, to stretch out the golden summer throughout the year.

Mary Campbell, who is an imaginative gardener and cook as well as writer, has her own kitchen garden beside her 200-year-old farmhouse in Salisbury, New Hampshire. Her delightful historical folklore, growing information, and the "virtues" of herbs have been carefully researched by the author and authenticated by T. H. Everett, Senior Horticulture Specialist of The New York Botanical Garden. The recipes and hints, some new, some old favorites, have been tested in The Betty Crocker Kitchens.

We hope you will find inspiration in these pages to plant and nurture, no matter how small, a garden of your own . . . to give a lift to your table *and* your life.

Betty Crocker

Chapter 1

From a Garden of Sallets to the Kitchen Garden

I content my felf then with an Humble Cottage, and
a simple *Potagere*,* Appendant to the Calendar.
—JOHN EVELYN (1620–1706)

IN THE EARLY PART of the seventeenth century, when Captain John
Smith was sailing along the coasts of New England charting their con-
tours, he landed on an island off Maine in the month of May and
planted there a "garden of sallets." These apparently were herbs and
vegetables suitable for making the fresh green salads so beneficial to
seagoing men. Within the next few months, he returned to the island
and harvested his "sallets" whenever he could.

You can hardly call Captain Smith's garden a kitchen garden, but
it was as close as he could come to one. Perhaps "galley garden" would
be a more appropriate name. It is sure that cook and men aboard Captain Smith's ship welcomed the fresh green additions to the ship's
daily fare.

When the Pilgrims and the Puritans landed and the settlers of James-
town and New Amsterdam and many other places along the eastern
seaboard first arrived, tiny "kitchin gardens" of herbs and small vegetables for use as food were planted as soon as possible in the dooryards
of the primitive homes. These men and women had brought with them
a few cherished seeds and plants for sustenance in an unknown world
of unknown hazards. They brought vegetable and grain seeds and

* *Potagere*, that is, a kitchen garden.

1

herbs for "physic, fragrance and flavor," of benefit to the health as well as the pleasure of the pioneers.

To their surprise they found the natives, whom they called "Indians" (as had others before them), tending fields of corn, pumpkins, beans, and squashes—substantial, nourishing foods that they were quick to adapt to their own uses. The Indians gathered from the woods many wild herbs for medicine and food, and shared with the white men their knowledge of the uses of these plants. Fields of wild strawberries grew along the coasts, and other wild berries in abundance could be found in almost every area. Many of these plants grow in the kitchen gardens of today.

In those early days, every housewife, lowly or grand, tended her own kitchen garden. The orchards, the fields of grain and staple foods, and most of the farm animals required the attention of her husband. But it was the wife's job to see to the planting, tending, and harvesting of the small vegetables used in her kitchen. She also had to know the medical and culinary uses of herbs, which she knew were essential to the health of her own family and neighbors. Like the monks of old, the prudent early American housewife shared with the sick and the poor who came to her door the medical lore and the goodness and the plenty of her garden. Even Martha Washington was responsible for the planting and care and dispensing of the products of her kitchen garden at Mount Vernon. Mrs. Washington walked along its fragrant paths checking on the progress of each valuable herb plant, each vegetable row or espaliered fruit tree, even guarding the welfare of the honeybees happily busy within the productive walled area. Now restored to its original appearance and condition, the Mount Vernon garden is a perfect example of a bountiful kitchen garden.

Not everyone is privileged to have so well ordered a garden or as much space as Mrs. Washington had. But the gardening instinct rises within almost everyone who owns a piece of land. This instinct may be deepest among those who own only as much land as can be crowded into a flowerpot or a boxful of soil on a sunny windowsill or under special lights in a dark hallway. But even so small a garden is invaluable if you appreciate fresh crisp vegetables and herbs for cooking when they are at their peak of flavor and succulence. The close relationship between eating and gardening makes it desirable for good cooks to gather the freshest products for the kitchen from their own dooryards.

"The kitchen garden is the best of all gardens" is an old adage. The kitchen garden is a home garden in which you may grow vegetables and herbs (and sometimes fruits) for use as food. It is small enough to be cultivated with hand tools. It is easily accessible from the kitchen or back door of the house to save steps and to prevent wet feet when it rains. It need not be large to provide a succession of greens and vegetables for your table. A plot the size of a dining-room rug (nine feet by twelve feet, or ten by fifteen) can provide a family of as many as four with at least one fresh vegetable every day during the entire season, taking advantage of succession plantings. The same garden can supply many of the herbs your family is likely to need during the year. Such a garden is worthy of careful planning for practical use and enjoyment.

A kitchen garden may provide fresh seasonings for every month of the year; even when it is covered with light snow, sage, winter savory, and parsley can be garnered. If your garden is large enough, you may find that it will provide herbs and vegetables in such abundance that you will never need to buy these foods. However, bearing in mind that the simple garden is the easiest to care for, if you are a *beginner* keep the first garden small. If you begin with an herb patch four feet square you will probably want to stretch that tiny space to include more favorites as each new planting season arrives.

For gardens have a way of growing larger with each new year. Herbs and vegetables grow enthusiastically, as if eager to add their bounty to our tables. They are extremely easy to grow, taking much more neglect than should be expected of them. The gardener who dreams of great harvests is also enthusiastic. It is wise to start in a small, simple way and let the garden expand with your experience and needs. Better to plant not quite enough the first year than to waste time, space, and food; all are equally valuable.

Gardens and gardening satisfy some of our most basic needs, both in spirit and flesh. Working with growing things, in the sunshine and fresh air and privacy of our own gardens, genuinely lifts the spirits. The more crowded the country, the more valuable it is to make a garden a part of your daily life, enjoyed for its beauty, for comfort, and for use. There are so many virtues in gardens. Each new sprout in the new springtime of each year is an exciting disclosure. Each green leaf, filled with valuable minerals and vitamins, promotes good health and well-being. And do you know any place on earth where there is more peace and quiet and contentment than in your own garden? Where else are such recreation, good health, and economy so pleasurable, so rewarding for the whole family? Where else are the senses so tantalized by the flavor and fragrance of fresh-picked herbs, the feeling of crisp, tender leaves, the sight of well-ordered and beautiful growing things?

Cookbooks today include hundreds of recipes that call for the use of herbs. This is for one reason—herbs make food taste better, whether prepared by beginning, experienced, or "gourmet" cooks. Herbs make preparation of meals more exciting and more flavorful, not to say more healthful.

The dictionary says that a gourmet is a connoisseur in eating and drinking who discriminatingly appreciates differences in flavor or quality. A "gourmet cook" might be defined as one who uses herbs and wine with taste and flair. But even for the everyday three-meals-a-day busy mother of a hungry family, using home-grown herbs and vegetables will add to the fun and pleasure of cooking. Only from one's own kitchen garden, be it indoor or outdoor, large or small, can such fresh green fare be chosen.

> A little garden in which to walk, and immensity in
> which to dream. At one's feet that which can be
> cultivated and plucked; overhead that which one can
> study and meditate upon: some [herbs] on earth,
> and all the stars in the sky.
>   —VICTOR HUGO (1802–1885)

Chapter 2

The Plan Is the Beginning

Gentlemen of the better sort and quality will provide . . .
a parcell of ground to bee laid out for their [kitchen]
garden and in . . . convenient manner. To prescribe one forme
for every man to follow were too great presumption
and folly: for every man will please his own fancie.
—John Parkinson (1567–1650)

Thoughts of springtime and gardens begin creeping into our day-dreams when the busy days of Christmas are over and winter has closed in. This is the best possible time for planning the kitchen garden. The seed and garden catalogs begin to arrive, and their colorful pictures tempt us to search out pages of ideas for planting, new developments in plants, new vistas of summer enjoyment and fall harvests.

It is true, as Mr. Parkinson says, that each man's garden is unique, his very own. As a gardener you grow those things that you like best, if they are suited to the climate and soil. Experimenting with both the growing and the culinary uses is part of the joy of the kitchen garden, but you ought to plan from the beginning to grow those things you will enjoy, best utilizing the space and the time you have available.

If you keep a record from the beginning of the kitchen garden planning, planting, and harvesting you will make your tasks easier in succeeding seasons. Pencil and notebook at hand, measure the garden to scale; study the seed and plant catalogs; learn how to plant and harvest; choose the plants; and your dream begins to unfold on paper.

An important purpose of making any garden plan is to enhance the whole picture of your home. House, garden, and owners should all be compatible elements and seem to belong together. One of the considerations in bringing about this happy relationship is the architecture of your house. A large formal house calls for a formal garden laid out in straight lines and beds of substantial size and regular shape. An informal house may have naturalized gardens, with curving borders and asymmetrical planted areas. Whatever their size or shape, gardens should be easy to reach and maintain, well-groomed, weed-free, and pleasantly orderly. The smaller the garden, the more important is this neatness.

Few plants fit into diverse architectural qualities of house and landscape as well as the herbs. They are completely at home in the formal beds of great estates, and equally so in informal surroundings. They blend perfectly with old-fashioned New England houses, with ground-hugging modern ranch houses, with skyscrapers in penthouse or roof gardens. Furthermore, they flourish like weeds in a wide variety of climates. They are truly the most adaptable, amenable, even charming, plants there are. If you can discard old-wives' beliefs that vegetables are only utilitarian, and learn to see them for what they are—plants of great beauty, texture, and color—you will realize that they, too, fit into all these landscape pictures with ease.

There is no reason why herbs and vegetables should not fit very well into an already existing garden pattern, either added to flower beds or in separate beds. The shapes, textures, and foliage colors of many kitchen garden plants add variety to flower-garden and lawn areas, and herbs in particular add fragrance to a pleasure garden. Lettuce, cabbage, or kale, for example, add rounded shapes and varied color in a low border. The green lacy foliage of carrots adds interest to the massed color of annuals such as petunias. Spiky leaves and delicate flowers of chives outline any garden area attractively and provide interesting as well as useful borders.

As Mr. Parkinson gently points out, no rules will cover *all* gardeners' needs and wishes. However, two rather traditional garden designs may guide the planning. Both of these plans contain some important herbs and small vegetables. These are suggestions to provide interest and inspiration for the beginning gardener in adapting the kitchen garden of your choice to your own home. Your needs, time, and space will suggest your own changes in these designs. If the designs do not suit a presently existing garden plan, the pages that follow will help you choose plants for tucking into corners of the flower beds, for bordering walks, for enhancing the dooryard. You can make a choice of plants to be used as accents in pots on a terrace; or in a jewel-box city garden hidden behind a row house; or for plantings in pots or window boxes in a sunny window if you are an aspiring gourmet cook who lives in a city apartment. If there is plenty of space in your dooryard, you will have few planting problems. If your plot of land is contained in a small box of soil your plantings must be limited to a precious few, but you will find yourself no less devoted to these few favorites.

One such small kitchen garden, in an alleyway, takes up no more space than two feet by six feet on each side of the gate, providing room for the plants which its intrepid gardener feels are essential to her: cucumbers on the fence, two plants of rhubarb and a plum tree, and nasturtiums and parsley in a gay border along the edge.

The lay of the land will govern the size and shape of your kitchen garden. A sloping terrace, especially one facing south, lends itself to herb and vegetable plantings, perhaps interspersed with colorful annual flowers for gaiety and variety. The problems of an oddly shaped property are often solved by kitchen garden plantings that might include the clever use of fencing (ah, the neighbors' dogs!) or trellising for vines such as cucumbers or beans or grapes. Accents of staked tomatoes or herbs in containers fill many awkward garden areas.

So you may stand in the doorway and look straight through to the end of the yard, visualizing the garden as you would like it to be, the plantings arranged for convenience as well as beauty. This dream should result in a single picture of good design that will be useful and restful for your family's greatest enjoyment.

Although kitchen garden plants in general are adaptable, they are fussy about a few requirements, and these needs cannot be ignored. The three most important needs of herbs and vegetables are good loamy soil, good drainage, and usually sunshine.

If the soil in your garden is not good, you can probably improve

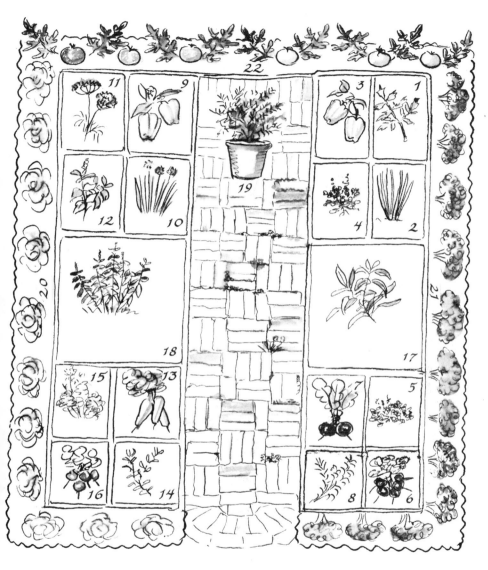

1. Lovage
2. Garlic
3. Peppers
4. Marjoram
5. Thyme
6. Radishes
7. Beets
8. Tarragon
9. Peppers
10. Chives
11. Dill
12. Basil
13. Carrots
14. Tarragon
15. Chervil
16. Radishes
17. Sage
18. Mint
19. Rosemary
20. Lettuce
21. Parsley
22. Tomatoes

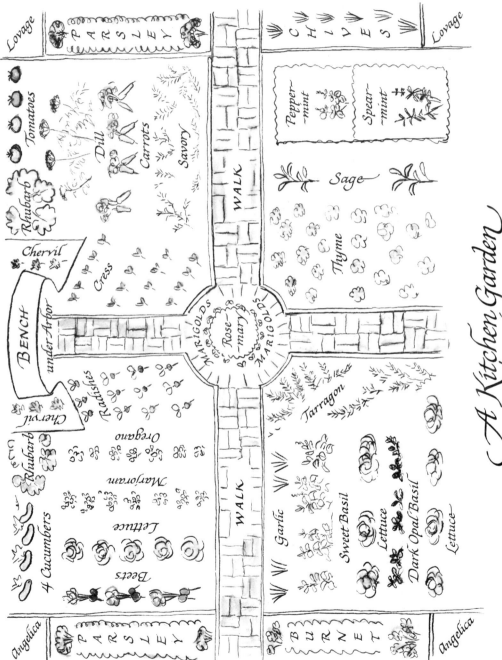

A Kitchen Garden

it; almost any soil can be made productive. Preparation of the soil is treated in its own section (see page 14).

Good drainage is essential, because kitchen garden plants will not tolerate wet feet. A south-facing slope provides both good drainage and needed sunshine. Lacking this, almost any other area of the garden where water does not stand in puddles, where tree roots and deep shade do not exist, where cold winds do not directly strike the plants, will produce an excellent kitchen garden. If necessary to provide drainage, you can easily create raised beds, using boards or tiles to provide the "box" of soil for such beds. Fences, walls, or sides of buildings provide effective protection against cold and wind.

Tall plants are best placed so that they do not crowd or shade smaller plants. Annuals should be conveniently planted together so that their comings and goings will not disturb the roots of the perennials. All plants should be arranged so that they can be reached easily for maintenance and harvesting. But, somehow, even if these conditions are difficult to provide, kitchen garden plants seem to grow.

Because the ideal kitchen garden is to be enjoyed as well as used, try to provide pleasant walks or paths. Depending on the architecture of house and general landscaping, you have a wide choice of path materials. Grass might be most suitable and the easiest to maintain; if so, the paths between beds must be wide enough to accommodate the lawn mower. Bricks, flagstones, marble chips, or shredded bark may be attractive. You could have a bench in a quiet corner and perhaps a sundial to count the sunny, happy hours or a birdbath to invite its useful visitors.

The plan is the beginning. Knowing how to plant is the next step in an exciting adventure.

> My Garden sweet, enclosed with walles strong,
> Embanked with benches to sitt and take my rest;
> . . . The arbores and alyes so pleasant and so dulce.
> —*An Elizabethan Gardener*

Chapter 3

With Spade and Rake and Hoe

... and such gardens are not made
By singing:—"Oh how beautiful!"
and sitting in the shade.
   —RUDYARD KIPLING (1865–1936)

THE PLANTING

FOR ABOUT FIFTY CENTS—the price of several postcards—you may have a wealth of garden information at hand in the catalogs of seedsmen, nurserymen, and herb growers. Their pages are rich in descriptions and pictures of plants and their characteristics, planting dates, and growing requirements. Not every catalog will contain all the information or list all the seeds and plants that you may require, so it is good practice to be on the mailing list of a number of seedsmen. Ordering something once a year suffices to keep your name on the mailing lists. Advertisements in gardening magazines usually are a reliable source of names and addresses of seed and plant specialists. (A partial listing has been made for convenience on pages 165–166 of this book.)

Experienced gardeners rely on their own judgment for such climatological facts as frost-safe planting and harvesting dates. If you are a beginning gardener, you may be able to get this information from an experienced neighbor (flattered that he should be asked). Or you may wish to consult your county agricultural agent, or the state agricultural college, or write to your Congressman in Washington for information on weather dates supplied by the United States Department of Agriculture. Sometimes local areas differ from the normal climate, depending on altitude, proximity to large bodies of water, or other

13

unusual factors. Gardening weather may be fickle, and gardens located a hundred yards apart will sometimes have differing frost susceptibility.

PREPARATION OF THE SOIL

Most herbs and small vegetables require a "sweet" or alkaline soil, which means some lime content. To determine whether the soil is suitably alkaline for the kitchen garden, you can buy small inexpensive home soil-testing kits from most seedsmen, either from catalogs or at local garden-supply shops. Using them is a simple experiment in chemistry that can be a lesson for the whole family. Soil tests will also be made by most state agricultural agents or colleges. If the garden soil is acid, the right degree of sweetness may be achieved by adding to it ground limestone, wood ashes, or discarded eggshells slightly crushed (they break down even more in the soil). Fireplace ashes are especially valuable for this purpose. In many homes, especially in New England, the ashes are left banked in the fireplace until spring, when the fireplaces are cleaned out and the heap of ashes is strewn on the gardens, as has been done for over three hundred years. The soil test may also determine what chemical and organic elements are lacking in the garden soil.

You should aim for a loamy texture in the garden soil, achieved by a well-balanced mixture of clay, compost or manure (or in their absence, peat moss or leaf mold), and sand. In such soil, almost anything will grow and flourish. Roots find it difficult to penetrate heavy soils consisting of wet sticky clay, and clay soil retains moisture, so that plants are often waterlogged and the roots are unable to breathe or grow. Compost or well-rotted manure lightens this type of soil, provides natural fertilizers, and allows breathing space for the roots. Organic gardeners enthusiastically endorse such soil treatment. In addition to the compost (or manure), sand is also useful to provide lightness and good drainage. Clay soil generally requires the addition of lime in some form.

If the soil is so sandy that it is always dry in growing seasons, it will be easy to work, but the plants will suffer in times of drought, and the garden will require special watering attention. In addition, sandy soil is so porous that fertilizer quickly leaches out of it, leaving the growing garden without sustenance. Here again, the addition of abundant compost, peat moss, or leaf mold will help to create the desired loamy texture, with lime and bone meal for sweetening and enriching.

Soil can be improved greatly by the addition of plenty of organic matter. Well-rotted barnyard manure, of course, is the very best soil enricher there is. Its two chief drawbacks are that it may be unavailable to the average gardener, and that it contains weed or grass seeds in some quantity. Dried cow manure is safe and excellent to use in place of barnyard manure, with the added advantages of being easily available (though somewhat expensive), easy to handle, and free of weed seeds. You should use it together with the next best conditioners, which are compost, leaf mold, or peat moss.

ABOUT COMPOST

My bank boasts no president,
   nor board of directors,
Nor books, nor bricks,
   nor IBM correctors,
Nor debits, nor credits,
   nor calendared statements,
Nor checks, nor interest,
   nor audit abatements.

But its treasury is rich
   in mineral savings,—
Of eggshells and peelings
   and old garden shavings,
Of soil and toil and
   brown leaves and mold.
My compost pile
   is pure garden gold.

For those gardeners not fortunate enough to have plenty of manure available to enrich their soil (and that means most of us), a compost pile, which may be as small as three feet wide by three feet deep by six feet long, is the most valuable source of enrichment. Where well-made compost is used, chemical fertilizers may not be necessary except perhaps for forcing. Compost is the basis of organic gardening, that is, gardening with the use of plant materials that have been broken down into humus and fertilizer by the action of natural living organisms.

Compost is made up of layers of soil; vegetable matter such as green weeds, grass clippings, tops of garden plants, coffee and tea grounds, fruit rinds and vegetable peelings, pea pods, corn husks; and an occasional application of lime or wood ashes. Wood ashes should never be thrown away. They are invaluable additions to the garden and to compost. Leaves that are raked from the gardens in fall and spring add special nutrients; it is a waste to burn them or otherwise destroy them. It has been said that among weeds, green dandelions and nettles are two of the most beneficial additions to compost, not only enriching it with natural components, but hastening the decomposition and fermentation of the pile (this is true, however, of any herbaceous leaves and stems). Nevertheless, adding them to the pile will rid the garden of two sometimes troublesome occupants, and you can add their fellow weeds as well.

Compost will in time decay by itself, but it takes a year or even two for it to decompose enough to use in the garden. The addition of some activator is therefore necessary. Barnyard or hen manure is excellent. You may purchase a specially prepared organic mixture at small cost in garden-supply shops that will hasten the decomposition of the whole compost stack when applied as directed. You can then use the decayed matter on the garden within a few months.

The stack should be made up in layers like a *torte:* first, waste vegetable matter, then a layer of soil or manure if available, another layer of vegetable matter, then soil, or sand, a sprinkling of lime or ashes, the commercial activator if necessary, and so on. Keep the pile moist (by occasional watering when needed) to assist the fermentation process, and turn it over with a garden fork two or three times during the gardening season. Do not add meat scraps of any kind to the compost pile, for they may attract unwanted animals.

When properly prepared, the product that results from the decay of the compost is rich in nutrients for the garden, and it improves any kind of soil. It makes an excellent mixture for potting plants for the house and the garden, for seed flats, cold frames, and greenhouse use. And it costs almost nothing, a perfect example of how to conserve and put to use household waste to make any conservationist smile.

Searching at country auctions, you may be lucky enough to find an old-fashioned hand-operated fodder chopper (now considered to be an antique tool), which cuts vegetable matter into small pieces, thus greatly hastening decomposition. Electric and gasoline shredders on the market also do an excellent job of chopping the leaves and stems of plants. If your kitchen garden and flower gardens are large enough, this investment would pay for itself in a few years by saving the cost of chemical fertilizers, soil conditioners, or loads of manure. The chopper turns out a fine product that decomposes much more rapidly than unchopped material.

Compost piles should not be located under coniferous trees because of the slight retarding action of dripping gum and turpentine and because rainfall may not reach them there to keep them moist. Otherwise, they can be located in any out-of-the-way place in a garden, behind shrubs or a fence or a building. They can even be made in a hole dug several feet deep into the ground. A pile of the dimensions already mentioned is easily managed and provides sufficient compost for the average garden. Half the space provided can be filled with fresh materials in layers while the rest of the pile (which has decomposed) is being used. The half-piles alternate in being stacked and being used. Chicken-wire frames, cement blocks, tiles, bricks, or boards make sturdy sides to keep the pile neat and easy to manage.

Many small gardeners and indoor gardeners have neither the space nor the materials with which to make compost. For them packaged peat moss, dried cow manure, bone meal, and commercial fertilizers are especially convenient. Bone meal is a natural fertilizer and is safe to use because it acts slowly and does not burn plants. A "balanced" commercial fertilizer having a formula of 5-10-5, which means 5 percent nitrogen, 10 percent available phosphoric acid, and 5 percent available potash, is the best to use for most gardens, unless the soil test suggests a higher proportion of one of these elements.

The best time to begin preparation of garden soil is in the fall. Sods can be removed at this time. If barnyard manure is available to furnish both soil conditioner and fertilizer, you can apply it fresh in the fall, but not in the spring or it will burn the seedlings. If manure is lacking, add compost (or peat moss or leaf mold). If you apply bone meal as a fertilizer in the fall, by spring it will be ready to help the plants with their growing problems.

A garden that is approximately ten feet by fifteen feet—that dining-room rug size—will appreciate the addition of six or more wheelbarrow loads or bushel baskets full of whatever conditioner is used. You can hardly apply too much. Spade the chosen area deeply and leave it roughly turned over until spring. The alternate freezing and thawing, and the rains, snows, and winds of winter's weather will be of great help in improving the texture of the soil and making it ready for spring planting.

If it is impractical to prepare the garden in the fall, start in the spring by adding the dressings mentioned above and follow the same steps, remembering that barnyard manure in the spring *must* be well rotted to avoid damage to new plants. You may safely apply dried cow manure, available in large and small quantities in convenient sized bags

from garden shops (and even supermarkets), in the spring. The smell is evident for a few days, as is that of barnyard manure, but think of its value to the soil and the odor will seem earthy and good.

You may dig in commercial fertilizer with the soil (according to directions on the bag) when preparing the garden in the spring. You may also use it as a side-dressing, applied along the rows or dug into the soil around individual plants. Do not apply it closer to the plants than two or three inches, or it may burn them, and for the best results put it on just before a rain or water it in well with a hose.

This is not as complicated as it sounds. It is just that soil to be good for gardens generally needs the addition of a conditioner, such as manure, compost, peat moss, or leaf mold; some fertilizer, such as manure or compost (or bone meal or commercial fertilizer); and a sweetener, such as lime or wood ashes.

When the warm days of spring arrive, wait until the soil is friable (which means that when a handful of soil is squeezed it crumbles easily, falls apart, and does not stick together like bread dough). Then study the kitchen garden plan, mark off the boundaries, and with spade and rake and hoe ready the planting beds. Apply the conditioners and fertilizer, and scatter the bone meal and ashes or lime according to soil tests or your own good judgment. (A wise lady once said, "If you haven't good judgment you'll never make a good cook or anything else.") Lightweight tools make the job easy. The spade goes in deep; the soil turns over, rich and fragrant. Rake out the sticks and roots and stones and rocks, and smooth the seedbeds. Smell the good earth. Enjoy the look of smooth, clean seedbeds, ready for delicate seeds and plants.

Gardens are easier to maintain if the beds are edged. You can make a straight cut all around each bed with a sharp straight spade and put an edging in place. Cedar boards make satisfactory boundary edgings; bricks are attractive and easy to handle. You can buy metal edgings for this purpose and sink them to ground level so that the metal is unobtrusive to sight and lawn mower; they are effective in keeping a clean edge on all beds and can be bent for curved borders.

As a guideline for planting rows, you can use a straight board, which

is easy to stand on while preparing the seed rows so that you do not step
into the smoothly raked soil, and is easy to shift from row to row. Some
gardeners like to use a string and two stakes. Your choice.

SOWING THE SEEDS

Excellent directions for the appropriate time and method of sowing
seeds of herbs and vegetables will be found in the catalogs and on the
seed packets. It is good to remember that there is life in each tiny
pellet and none should be wasted. If you sow too freely in order to
empty your packet at once you may find that a cold wet season will
produce no seedlings and you may have to reseed. Other hazards await
newly sown seeds, too. An old gardener's rhyme tells us to sow—

> Two for the cutworm, one for the crow,
> One for the beetle, and four to grow.

Sowing carefully according to directions on the packets will produce fine plants without waste. Several crops of some herbs and vegetables will be planted in succession (see page 23) during a single season,
so seeds that are not used in the first planting can be saved for such
later plantings. Some seeds remain viable (capable of producing life)
for several years.

There is seldom much to be gained by sowing seeds while there is
still a risk of frost and cold weather. Neither herb nor vegetable seeds
respond until their proper planting time arrives—when the ground
and weather are ready.

In order that plants get the maximum of sunlight while growing,
rows generally should run north and south. With a hoe you can make
shallow drills or furrows in which to sow the seeds. If the soil and
weather are very dry, it is well to water the drill before sowing the
seed. Old wives sowed their seed "three times their depth," and this is a
good rule of thumb to remember. Very tiny seeds need only to be
dropped into the drill and pressed down; larger seeds should be sown
and then covered with fine earth or sand. After sowing and covering
the seeds, tamp the row with a small board, or the back of the hoe, or
with your foot, to firm the soil.

When sowing succession plantings in the heat of summer, plant seeds a little more deeply and water them gently.

The earliest plantings in your kitchen garden will be of peas, lettuce, and radishes. Closely following will be onions, carrots, beets, leeks, parsley, and dill. Wait until after the last frost for sowing most other seeds, except those that are to be started earlier indoors.

STARTING SEEDS INDOORS

If you are a beginning gardener, you may find it easy to buy plants of some herbs and vegetables that are slow growing or perennial, those that must be started a month or two ahead of the warm planting season. When you become more adventuresome, you may want to grow these plants yourself by starting them on a sunny windowsill or under lights at the appropriate time. It is much more fun than buying someone else's plants and saves money that might be spent elsewhere more enjoyably.

Many herbs, annual as well as perennial, and such vegetables as tomatoes, peppers, and cucumbers may be started indoors to get a head start on the season. "Two months before apple blossom time" was the old rule. Seeds may be sown in flats, boxes, or pans three to four inches deep; or in individual pots; or in the newly available and excellent peat pellets, which are a great modern gardening aid. These are compact, flat, dried peat wafers that expand when watered to become small planting containers filled with planting medium. Two or three seeds may be sown into each wafer and thinned to one plant when the second set of leaves develops. As the plant grows, the roots grow thickly into the wafer, and it may be put into the soil after danger of frost without disturbing the roots. The wafers provide a sterile planting medium that eliminates the fatal mildew or fungus disease called "damping-off" that often attacks seedlings growing in ordinary soil. When planting these miniature pots in the garden, very gently break the net surrounding the expanded wafer to enable the roots to adjust to the surrounding soil and water conditions. The plants will then perform better.

Pots made of dried peat, which must be filled with fine potting soil mixed with sand, are also available. After planting the seeds, keep the pots damp, and as with the wafers, set them into the ground. In planting these pots, tear the sides of the pots carefully, again helping the roots to adjust to the new planting conditions. Such pots eliminate one step of the early seeding and growing process—that of transplanting from flat into a larger flat or pot and then into the soil. They also produce better plants, with no transplanting setback, because the roots are not disturbed when the plants are set out in the garden.

If planting seeds in flats, fill the box to within one-half inch of the top with potting soil consisting of two-thirds sifted compost and soil (or commercial potting soil), one-third sand. Firm with a small board, make a furrow "three times the depth" of the seed, and sow as directed on the packet. Cover lightly with fine soil or sand, water carefully so as not to wash the seed out of its nest, and cover the box with a piece of glass or plastic wrap. When the seeds begin to sprout, remove the covering immediately and put the box in a warm sunny place on a windowsill. Fluorescent lights have been devised for indoor gardeners that make easy work of raising seedlings indoors where sunny windowsills are in short supply (see pages 126–127, "The Little Gardens").

When the second pair of leaves appear, it is time to transplant the seedlings from flats to individual pots. Then keep them in a warm and sunny place and water when needed until time to transplant into the garden. Turn the plants a little each day to avoid leggy growth, which means they are reaching to find the sun. The plants may be hardened off in preparation for planting in the garden by setting them out of doors on warm days to become acquainted with life in the open.

TRANSPLANTING INTO THE GARDEN

> This rule in gardening do not forget:
> Always sow dry and set wet.
> —*From an old Almanac*

In order to lessen the shock for the plants when moving them into the garden, either set them into the soil on cloudy—even rainy—days, or shelter them from the sun and wind for a day or two with shingles, old strawberry boxes, or paper cones, until their roots become established. Otherwise, they will be subjected to heat and light that will wilt them and retard their growth. This is especially true of seedlings grown in flats or bought from commercial growers in boxes, because the roots are disturbed in planting.

With a trowel, dig a hole large enough to hold all the roots without crowding, pour water into the hole, set in the plant carefully, and firm the soil well (but gently) with your fingers. If desired, place additional compost around the plant as a kind of mulch and for future feeding. Or give the plants a light application of balanced commercial fertilizer, not too close to the tender stems and roots. "Manure tea" is a favorite starter for some gardeners. You can make it by putting a shovelful of manure in the bottom of an old five-gallon bucket or can, adding water to the brim, and allowing the mixture to stand overnight. A half cup or cup of this concoction is very helpful to give transplants a boost when they are set into the garden.

SUCCESSION PLANTINGS

Let nothing be lost!
—*Farmer's Almanack*

In order not to waste any of the precious space in the kitchen garden, and to insure a continuing supply of produce during the growing season, you should make "succession plantings." Time a second sowing (usually a week or two later) so that as soon as one crop matures and has been consumed—radishes or lettuce, for example—the second sowing is ready for eating. You can put thinnings from a row of another plant into the spaces that have been emptied, or sow seeds directly. For economy of space and work, the garden should have no fallow areas. This diversified use of planting areas keeps the garden fully productive, conserves space, helps prevent growth of weeds, and benefits the soil.

Quick-growing herbs and vegetables that are suitable for succession plantings are lettuce, radishes, garden cress, basil, dill, beets, carrots, and early beans.

COMPANION PLANTS

A whole new picture of plant growth may be emerging with the study of "companion" plants. Some gardeners believe that some plants have natural affinities with their neighbors in their relationships to each other, their environment, and their uses. This might be a fascinating subject to explore, and an eager kitchen gardener will want to learn about all the possibilities to assure success in growing plants as well as in using them. For example, do peas and carrots have a natural affinity for each other that makes them perform better if planted close together in the garden? Although there is little scientific proof as yet, proponents of "plant symbiosis" also declare that some plants may be antagonistic when planted near each other. Cabbage and strawberries do not make good neighbors in the garden, they say; neither do they blend well at table, of course; tomatoes and fennel are not on garden speaking terms. They declare that lettuce, on the contrary, is such a good neighbor that it enhances many things growing near it, especially radishes, carrots, strawberries, and onions. Do chives growing under apple trees really discourage the growth of apple scab? It has also been believed that chives help to repel insects in the garden.

Most herbs enjoy being near other plants in some way, but basil and rue are old enemies, as Nicholas Culpeper pronounced in his herbal over three centuries ago, and neither thrives when planted near the other. It has long been said that garlic planted under rosebushes thrives mightily and so do the roses; but garlic should not be planted too close to peas.

Nettle, that troublesome weed so despised by persons with sensitive skin, is said to benefit plants growing near it; it has been believed to have almost magical powers in helping nearby tomatoes to resist spoiling. If it is seen growing in raspberry patches producing berries of unsurpassed size and flavor, is it the nettles or the rich soil that cause this superiority? Thrown on the compost pile, nettle plants very well may stimulate the formation and fermentation of the humus, as companion plant enthusiasts say, and add valuable chemical properties to the compost (as do many other plants, of course). Do not despise the dynamic stinging nettle until more is known about it. Remember Grandmother's belief in the power of marigolds to rid the garden of pests? This was long considered a foolish fantasy, an old-wives' tale. Now many botanists agree that marigolds do prevent some pest invasions.

If some plants in the kitchen garden flourish more than others, a study of "go-togethers" may provide the answer to the unusually lush growth and superior flavor. If some plants do not flourish even though the soil conditions are excellent, the weather is perfect, and maintenance is flawless, it may be that they are inhibited by their plant neighbors. There is still much to learn about plant symbiosis, and you can be your own Sherlock Holmes in this field.

GOOD GARDEN-KEEPING

Weeds, before going to seed, are far better in the compost pile than in the garden, where they deprive the cultivated plants of moisture, food, light, and space. When they appear in the garden, remove them carefully by hand or with a hoe so as not to disturb the roots of the cultivated plants. The best time to do this is after a rain or watering, when the soil is soft and gives up the weed easily to a gentle pull. After weeding, when the soil is just nicely damp, a mulch of compost, dried grass clippings, or soft hay, about two inches deep, will help to conserve the moisture in the soil and to keep down weed growth. Do not use fresh grass clippings because they heat while decomposing and may burn some plant roots. Dried clippings are excellent.

Herbs are not very popular with insects. Except for an occasional parsley worm or tomato worm, which do not constitute an "insect invasion" and should not be viewed with alarm, insects do not regularly inhabit a kitchen garden in which herbs are planted. Many garden pests can be handpicked and dropped into a can of kerosene or alcohol or beer. An occasional shower bath with a cold spray from a garden hose often keeps plants free of red spider mites and aphids. A little flat dish of beer or thinned molasses placed at random under sheltering plants and sunk to the rim in the soil will attract slugs and cutworms to drown happily in it. These pests are not particular; the cheapest stale beer will do. A board or shingle placed somewhere along the row where slug damage is noted will provide daytime shelter for the slippery things (which come out for their depredations only in the dark). You can then turn the board over in the morning and remove the slugs or step on them.

Where you notice cutworm damage—that is, when plants seem to be cut off or chewed near the soil line for no apparent reason—dig carefully around the base of the plant with your finger and you will probably unearth the culprits. They are nasty little brown or green worms about a half inch to an inch long, usually curled up. Dig in wood ashes or lime around the base of individual plants or rows of plants and you will discourage slugs and cutworms.

It has been scientifically proven that a planting of marigolds in any garden will rid the soil of nematodes for a period of three years. Nematodes are tiny worms that feed on the roots of seedlings and other plants, causing them to die or be stunted. They are so miniscule that they are not noticed until the damage is done. Marigolds are the answer to nematodes.

Songbirds are the most important and helpful aides to pest problems in gardens and should be encouraged in all possible ways to inhabit the area. Other valuable helpers in doing away with harmful insects are frogs, toads, ladybugs, praying mantises, dragonflies, lizards, and even small garden snakes (harmless ones, of course). Earthworms are probably no help in fighting pests, but they help to lighten soil by their constant working through it while consuming composted material. Charles Darwin, the great British naturalist, once estimated that earthworms deposit about two tons of digested matter per acre per year—all to the good of the garden.

Mildew on garden plants may be forestalled if you give plants room and air in the garden and thus help the foliage to stay dry.

A spray of rosemary, lavender, or hyssop in the linen or woolen chest will help to keep out destructive insects. A spray of sage, tarragon, thyme, or tansy laid across growing cabbage plants will keep away the cabbage moths. Because your kitchen garden is composed of plants that will be used as food, it is not good practice to use any spray or

*"I content myself with a Humble Cottage
and a Simple Kitchen Garden."*

Be a good garden-keeper.

insecticides. If a spray must be used because of an unusual situation, one of the least harmful to humans is pyrethrum. It is made of herbs and is efficacious because it is absolutely lethal to insects that it touches.

Except in time of extreme drought, or in very dry areas, the kitchen garden that is well cultivated and mulched will need little extra watering. If the plants show evidence of wilting, and watering is then indicated, soak the garden thoroughly with the hose, letting the water run slowly throughout the entire garden. The tops of the plants will also then benefit from a brisk brief spraying with the spray nozzle of the hose, to freshen the leaves and to keep them clean. This is best done in the late afternoon when the sun is low, or very early in the morning.

Maintenance in the kitchen garden, once the planting is done, takes very little time and effort each week to keep edges trim, weeds eliminated, and lawn areas mown regularly. There is a deep pride in being a good garden-keeper.

Chapter 4

The Wholesome Harvests

A housewife coming in from the garden
with an apron stuffed full of succulent
variety is a pleasant sight.
> —*The Old Farmer's Almanac*

GATHERING HERBS FOR HARVEST

IN THE FOURTEENTH and fifteenth centuries abroad, and even in early America, the harvesting of herbs and vegetables was often accompanied by the chanting of verses or prayers or the muttering of spells. Fortunately today we can dispense with this kind of ceremony in our harvesting.

The kitchen garden harvest is carried on throughout the whole year. In winter, gather snippings from your windowsill herbs and dig gently under the snow for fresh green sprigs of parsley, winter savory, and sage. In spring, pick the lacy chervil leaves to use in salads, and pull the first crisp red radishes and lettuce thinnings and the spring green onions. In summer and fall, cut tarragon for vinegars and fish or fowl and for freezing; choose cucumbers for salads and pickling; gather long branches of herbs to be dried or frozen for winter; and can tomatoes for many winter meals. Yes, all through the year you will find some gathering of kitchen garden produce.

Although you gather snippings of the fresh herbs for use in the kitchen selectively in spring, summer, and fall, and a few precious bits from the windowsill in winter, you may also have to prepare for long cold months when few fresh greens are available. Then you may reach into the freezer for the stored flavor of summertime; or into the herb cupboard for the incomparable flavor of home-dried leaves and seeds.

You may find many of the articles needed for preparing harvested herbs by poking around in secondhand or antique stores. Smooth wooden paddles and cutting boards are useful all year round, and with them old-fashioned wood-handled paring knives with sharp blades that are easily honed. Wooden bowls will be helpful in crumbling and sifting herbs; old-fashioned coffee grinders, for mincing dried leaves. You may use small clean window screens for drying herbs, and amusing glass, pottery, china, or wood containers for growing potted herbs, or for storing them when dried. Old ginger jars and mustard pots make handsome herb containers arrayed on a shelf in the kitchen. Grandmother's brown or yellow pottery custard cups hold herb butters; pretty bottles make colorful herb vinegar cruets. Mortars and pestles, or adaptable "separates" may start you on a collection that is interesting as well as useful. Many handmade baskets can be used in gathering or drying herbs and harvesting vegetables, and they make excellent containers for decorative arrangements of pots or of fresh herbs and vegetables. And do find teacups that Grandmother might have used for the stimulating herb tea that she offered to any member of the family and the most distinguished guest.

Directions for harvesting and drying individual herbs have been given in their descriptions (see pages 39–84), but some general directions apply to nearly all culinary herbs. Fresh herbs may be frozen or dried at any time during the growing year. If you gather a surplus of herb foliage in the preparation of meals, put it into a small plastic sandwich bag and store it in a carton in the freezer for another day. Or dry it in the cooling oven after you have taken out the pie, roast, or bread (see page 150). Then put it with other surplus dried snippings into a small jar—the herb pot—and you will have a delightful mixture to use in many ways. The peak time for gathering herbs, however, is at the height of their flavor, fragrance, and abundance.

The very best time to harvest leaves of herbs *in quantity* is just before the flowers have opened, when they are in bursting bud. Because this peak flavor is somewhat dissipated by the light and heat of the midday sun (like flowers, herbs wilt when picked in the heat of the day), gather the herb leaves in the morning before the sun has warmed them but after the dew has dried. Take only those herbs that you can attend to immediately, for picking and then leaving them untended causes a marked deterioration of flavor and scent through loss of their volatile oils.

If the herbs are dusty, rinse them immediately with cool water (or, better, spray them with the hose the night before the gathering), and gently shake excess moisture from them. Discard any bruised, soiled, or imperfect leaves and stems.

Branches of most herbs may be cut back by about two-thirds their height two or three times during the summer; they like it, grow better, and the plants are more shapely because of it. The plants will then appreciate a little extra dose of manure tea or rich compost to help them recover quickly from their barbering. After their last shearing, perennial herbs should have time to fulfill new growth before winter. So do not harvest perennials after early September in the far North, or late September or early October in the South.

DRYING HERBS

The purpose of drying herb leaves is to retain as much of the fresh flavor, color, and fragrance as possible. To achieve this, you must take some care to process the leaves quickly or these special qualities will disappear. So it is well to avoid bruising the leaves, allowing them to lie in the sun or unattended after picking, or processing them too long.

As soon as you have washed the branches or leaves and excess moisture has evaporated, lay them out carefully and separately to dry thoroughly on small, clean window screens, or frames over which you have stretched cheesecloth. Put the herbs out of sunlight in a well-ventilated dry room, garage, shed, or attic. This method of drying is efficient for a large herb harvest.

Large herb leaves such as sage, basil, and mint will dry more rapidly if picked from the stems before drying on screens. In addition to the screen-drying method for small-leaved herbs, such as thyme, marjoram, or savory, you may choose to gather them in small light bunches and hang just until dry in a warm place. These small-leaved herbs are more easily stripped from their stems after drying.

For a moderate harvest, oven-drying of herbs is easy and quick. Spread the herbs out on trays, cooky sheets, or jelly-roll pans and put into a hot (around 375°–400° F.) oven, with the door left slightly ajar. Herbs dried in this manner must be *very* carefully watched (don't answer the telephone while you are doing this or you will end up with a fine batch of burned herbs). They must be removed only moments after putting into the oven, as soon as they are crisp. Such processing has been found to retain color and flavor much better than a long, slow processing. Parsley and small-leaved herbs are particularly easy to dry in this manner. Herbs should be allowed to cool a few minutes before crumbling and bottling to avoid moisture condensation in the tightly closed jars. If mustiness develops after storing, discard the herbs.

When all the leaves are crispy dry and crumble easily in the fingers, prepare them immediately for putting into their containers. Dried leaves may be left whole and then crumbled when being used; or if you

have large amounts put them through an old-fashioned coffee grinder and then into jars. They may also be coarsely hand-crumbled by rubbing them briskly between the palms of your hands; then the stiff bits of stem and leaf veins may be removed, as in hand-rubbed sage (see page 65). Mixtures for *fines herbes* (see page 146) may also be put together and run through the coffee grinder before being bottled. Dried sprigs for *bouquets garnis* (see page 145) may be assembled and tied into small squares of cheesecloth and kept in a tightly closed tin or jar. Carefully label and date all jars.

It is one of the pleasantest tasks of the summer to prepare dried herbs for winter storage. An aura of delicious fragrance permeates the air and hovers over you as you sit in the garden or on the porch sifting and crushing the dried leaves.

Herbs hanging from the rafters of old houses look charming and old-fashioned and contribute delicate fragrance to the atmosphere, but this is not the most satisfactory way of storing them for use in cooking. Once they are dried, if the herbs are allowed to hang for any length of time in the warm air of the house, the flavor dissipates within a few weeks and they gather dust. For kitchen use, herbs should always be processed and bottled as soon as dry. Still, they do look fetching thus displayed so it is pleasant to harvest some herb branches just for this purpose, without any intention of using them for cooking.

FREEZING HERBS

For freezing, snippets of fresh herbs do not need to be blanched like vegetables. Pick them in the morning before the sun gets too warm, and rinse them in cool water to remove dust. Discard any bruised, discolored, or imperfect leaves. You can then put the sprigs loosely into small plastic sandwich bags, with a wire twisted around the open ends to seal, and put the bags into a large plastic carton marked with the name of the herb. Or staple the little bags together so that you can remove one bag at a time from the group. For many herb growers with freezer space, these are the most satisfactory methods of storing herbs to retain the utmost freshness. Frozen herbs retain flavor for about six months. (Remember to date the bags or cartons.)

You cannot use herbs thus processed in whole sprigs for garnishing, because they wilt as soon as thawed. However, you can chop them while they are still frozen, or put them through a Mouli parsley grater, and then scatter the minced herbs on or in foods, just as you use dried or freshly picked finely minced herbs.

Small packets of *fines herbes* or *bouquets garnis* can be frozen easily, too. When you want them for cooking, the little plastic bags can be opened and the herbs spilled into the food just as if they were freshly picked. (On pages 145–146 there are suggestions for such mixes.)

HARVESTING HERB SEEDS

Herb seeds may be successfully harvested for use in planting in the spring, as well as for use in the kitchen. Remove them from the plant when ripe, but before they begin to shatter from the heads. This takes careful watching for the right moment. When that moment comes, cut the stem with seed heads and turn upside down into a paper bag. Hang the bag in a dry room or shed for a few days. Then shake the bag rather vigorously and the seeds will fall into the bottom of the bag. You may then spread them onto a tray and remove the chaff (often by blowing it away). Then put the seeds into jars, close the jars tightly to keep the seeds dry, and label the jars carefully with name and date. Although some seeds remain viable for longer periods, results are best if they are used within twelve months, whether for cooking or for planting.

Some of the seeds that it may be useful to save are parsley, caraway (which grows so plentifully in some areas in the wild, especially in the northerly states, that you may not have to grow it in the garden), sage, basil, and dill, either for next year's sowing or for cooking. Angelica seed should be sown in the ground immediately upon ripening, as it does not keep well. Let chervil self-seed in its own bed (and dill and parsley, too, if you wish). Many herb growers find that their own seed produces stronger and better-flavored plants than any seeds that they purchase.

Because today's vegetables are usually carefully bred horticultural selections, it is not satisfactory to save vegetable seeds.

HARVESTING VEGETABLES

Flavor o' Summer between your teeth,
And those at home to love you;
Hearth and a cellarful underneath,
And God and a roof above you!
            —HOLMAN F. DAY
         The Old Farmer's Almanac

There is no excitement that quite matches the harvesting of the first vegetables of the year from your kitchen garden. They may be leeks that have snuggled down into the soil over the winter and are ready to eat when the ground is free of frost in the spring. They may be radishes, sown seemingly only days before (actually three to four weeks) and ready for salad in a surprisingly short time. Radishes are best when young and crisp. If you let them grow too large, they become bitter and tough. What is left of the first planting you can then pull up and put on the compost pile; your second planting should surely be ready to eat.

Then you should have the first thinnings of crinkly, crisp, green lettuce leaves, young beet greens, and carrots and beets. In New England peas traditionally must be ready by the Fourth of July; in warmer sections of the country they are long gone by then. All the other vegetables you cherish most and have somehow found room for in the kitchen garden will follow in quick succession.

The best time to go into the kitchen garden is early in the day when the air is cool, but when the dew has dried on the foliage. Pick the freshest of vegetables, whether roots or fruits or leaves. At this time of day they are crisp and refreshed from the cool of the night, after a day of sunshine, and are full-flavored and rich. Some vegetables, such as radishes, carrots, and beets, are best harvested when young and not fully grown; "baby carrots" and "baby beets" are sweeter and need only brief cooking, and a generous basting with butter, to be delicious. Gather your peas and green beans when they are tender-green and well-filled, before the pods become fat and tough.

Corn, asparagus, and peas are unbelievably richer and sweeter if you pick them and bring them straight to the kitchen for immediate cooking and serving.

The best advice is to pick the vegetables when they are ready, a matter of some judgment and experience. For new gardeners, however, one mistake is an excellent teacher.

"—AND SO TO BED"

The earnest writer of an early-nineteenth-century book on gardening gives advice for putting the garden to bed in autumn that is sensible if somewhat pious: "*Now* prepare ground for planting or sowing in early spring; lay the earth in ridges, to expose it to the action of frost. Increase your store of treasure in compost-heaps. Treat your master well, if you happen to be a servant; treat your servant well, if Providence has made you a master. Be thankful to Heaven for the blessings of health, strength and freedom; and remember that a gardener's work is never done."

Putting the kitchen garden to bed is a pleasant cleaning up of the year's sowing and reaping, and you can take pride in leaving the productive earth neat and ready for next spring's first exciting days of planting.

When the harvest is done, pull up all annual plants—vegetables as well as herbs—and compost those parts which are inedible. Remove, clean, and store stakes and labels. A thick covering of compost and fresh manure on the garden at this time will be valuable in the spring. Bone meal put on in the fall acts slowly, and by spring it, too, will be ready to help fertilize the new plantings. If only commercial fertilizers are available, wait until spring to apply. Their value to the soil is lost over the winter. Spade these coverings roughly into the soil (although it is not necessary to "lay the earth in ridges") and leave until spring. This helps aerate the soil, kill insect larvae, and break up stubborn clods or particles of compost.

Some perennial herbs such as tarragon and thyme will appreciate extra mulch, hay, or evergreen branches tucked round them to help protect from ice and snow, and to prevent heaving of the plants during thaws. Cover parsley, sage, and winter savory plants, from which some snippings can be taken all winter, with peach or apple baskets or wooden boxes for protection from ice and heavy snow. You may paint the baskets green if you like them to be more attractive. To gather these herbs in winter, lift the basket, take desired snippings, then replace the basket and put a weight—a rock or brick perhaps—on top to keep the basket from blowing away in a winter storm.

"I am most pleased with the goodness," said Mr. Samuel Pepys in 1662. "And so to bed."

Chapter 5

The Kitchen Garden Herbs

What signifies knowing the Names, if
you know not the Natures of Things?
—*Poor Richard's Almanack*

IN MOST CASES, the herbs that we include in kitchen gardens are as old
as man. Their flavor, and fragrance, their gifts of good health and well-
being have intrigued men since the beginnings of the Garden of Eden.
The qualities of these herbs have always been mysterious. We still do
not completely understand them, but they interest and delight us no
less today than through the ages past.

Have you wandered into the yard of an abandoned school and been
tempted to nibble at the watercress cascading from the dilapidated
trough with its old spring? Have you walked down a country road and
been tempted to climb over old stone walls to poke around for sweet
woodruff or mint or caraway once planted by a bride with sprigs from
her mother's garden? Have you driven through villages of Sarah Orne
Jewett's Maine coast and been tempted to get out and search for
pennyroyal to comfort an aching head or a tired back? Have you
walked through the sagebrush (it is not a true sage) of the Great West
and thought of ancient monasteries where sage tea was given to prolong
life and bring wisdom? If you have not known such a special kind of
joy—brought by a faint fragrance on a warm summer's day or after
an autumn rain—the possibility of enjoyment is in your own garden.

Because herbs are so old, their history fills books with stories of uses,
lore, and magic far beyond a single volume's capacity to detail in full.
But to help you understand and use a few of the herbs most appreciated
today, some of the facts are telescoped into the following pages. The

choice of "A Baker's Dozen Sweet Herbs" is quite arbitrary, as are the following "Four for Good Measure." Among them, you should find a happy choice to plant in your kitchen garden for culinary and household purposes. For the really enthusiastic herb-lover, no list could be long enough.

No one knew the herbs better than the early herbalists, including John Gerard (1545–1611), Nicholas Culpeper (1616–1654), John Evelyn (1620–1706), and John Parkinson (1567–1650), from whose books come many amusing or interesting passages about individual herbs. These gentlemen often ascribed "Vertues" or "Virtues" to each plant to explain their uses and benefits, so descriptive a term that it has been respectfully borrowed for these pages.

A Baker's Dozen Sweet Herbs

SWEET BASIL

(Ocimum basilicum)
A tender annual

This is the herb which all authors are together by the
ears about, and rail at one another like lawyers.
—NICHOLAS CULPEPER (1615–1654)

Most authorities today *agree* that sweet basil is a fine herb, with a
clovelike spicy tang that gives it great popularity. A packet of basil
seeds sometimes produces several different kinds of plants: some may
have smooth and satiny leaves, some, curled and pebbly. The typical
sweet basil has bright light green leaves and small white flowers. All
basils are useful and aromatic. A variety called Dark Opal has its own
basil flavor and is a deep red color with pink-purple flowers. This variety
makes beautiful claret-red vinegar and is handsome in flower arrangements. In cooking it is interchangeable with the green basils. Other
varieties of basil include dwarfs and one with a slight lemon taste. Seeds
for the sweet and the Dark Opal (sometimes also called purple) basils
are most easily found.

PLANTING: At planting time, each little basil seed wishes it
were in its native warm Mediterranean region, for it does not like
cold wet soil. You may start the seed indoors in a warm place early in
spring; or plant it outdoors after the ground is well warmed. It usually
germinates quickly in warm soil. Thin the plants to about eight inches
apart. You can use the thinnings for cooking or transplant them to
another place in the garden, or dry them and put them into the herb
pot (see page 150) on the kitchen table. Basil is also rooted easily by
putting slips into water. In order to have a plant in the house for winter,
root a slip (or sow some seed in a pot) in August. If given proper light

39

Sweet Basil   *In the Garden*

and humidity, scarcely any herb grows so happily in the house in winter.

HARVESTING: It is good to harvest some basil for storage, but it is still better to keep a green plant in the house all winter. It is an attractive potted plant and likes a warm sunny window. If you snip out the first flower buds (this is true in the garden as well as in the house) the basil will grow bushy and will produce more leaves and branches. During a normal outdoor season, you may harvest three cuttings. Just before frost (it is very tender to frost), pull the whole plant up, cut off the root, and dry the leaves whole for winter use. Basil also takes well to freezing for storage. The best method is to put little sprigs —enough for one pot of stew, one salad, or one casserole—into plastic sandwich bags, then store them in the freezer in a larger plastic carton marked "basil."

Basil is a tender plant when picked. You should be careful not to bruise the leaves or delay too long when preparing them for drying or freezing, or they will simply turn black and be useless. So handle with

40

care, dry or freeze quickly, and *use* with care, too, for it is a strong herb.

VIRTUES: John Gerard said that the use of basil "maketh a man Merry and Glad," and so it does. It is almost a staple in Mediterranean cookery, with such an affinity for tomatoes that it is difficult to imagine an Italian tomato dish without its basil. It is also valuable when used in combination with other herbs (remembering always that it is strong and must be used lightly) in salads and sauces; with fish, poultry, or game; with beef, veal, lamb, and pork; in soups (pea or bean—a delight!), stews, and stuffings. Basil makes a delicious herb butter for use in omelets and soups and with cheese dishes. A touch of it enhances any canned or frozen vegetables. It is almost an all-purpose herb, but its real love is tomatoes—soup, cocktail, and broiled or fresh-sliced tomatoes from the kitchen garden. You will find it a good herb to experiment with, combining it with other herbs to make *fines herbes* (see page 146) for use in many dishes. It combines especially well with chervil.

Basil has been a kitchen garden herb for centuries. It once was used for "strewing" floors to keep them sweet and clean; for chasing away witches and flies and headaches. In Italy it is a symbol of love and fidelity.

CHERVIL

(*Anthriscus cerefolium*)
Hardy annual

The leaves of sweet Chervill are exceeding good,
wholesome and pleasant among other sallad herbs,
giving the taste of Anise seed unto the rest.
— JOHN GERARD (1545–1611)

This delicate lacy herb is blessed by a subtle spicy flavor with slight overtones of anise or licorice. It is at its best in salads, as Mr. Gerard suggests. It is highly valued by the French, who include it in *fines herbes* combinations. Its lacy foliage makes a pretty planting in the garden, and because its flavor is so delicate, you may use it generously, which means generous-sized beds for an ample supply. Chervil is short-lived, and thus continuous plantings will be necessary during the early spring, then later in the spring and in the fall for constant use. Once established, a bed of chervil will keep itself going for years if you allow some of the plants to go to seed. Otherwise, for best flavor pick the flowers off before blooming. Chervil fades, bleaches, and falters when planted in full sun, especially in summer and in hot climates, but it does like a half-shady cool bed. It has biennial qualities if planted in the fall, and such plantings often live over the winter, ready to use when the snow melts in spring.

PLANTING: Sow the seed where you want the plants to grow, for they do not transplant well. Thin the plants to about eight inches apart, by pinching them off at the roots rather than pulling them out, so as not to disturb remaining roots. If the soil is kept cool and moist, the plants will not go to seed so quickly and will last longer for cutting. Chervil grows satisfactorily on a cool half-shady windowsill in winter if several plants are planted in a large box or basket by themselves—one plant is not enough to provide all you will need in the kitchen.

HARVESTING: Chervil is harvested fresh from the garden during the growing season in spring, fall, and winter in most areas. Chervil's thin and fragile leaves almost disappear in drying for storage, and so does the flavor unless you handle the plants very carefully, so it is best to freeze them or keep them in the window garden. If you decide to freeze this thin-leafed herb you will need a substantial quantity of it. And remember that you cannot then use it for garnishing salads, because it loses its crisp freshness when thawed. Minced while still frozen, chervil gives a fresh flavor to *fines herbes* combinations, used in salad dressings and on meats or fish.

VIRTUES: This delightful herb benefits nearly every dish you use it in. Its flavor is best when it is not cooked, or is cooked very little,

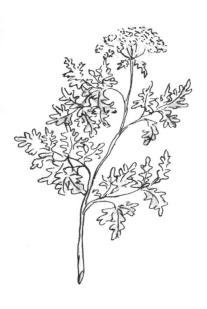

Chervil

In the Garden

so add it at the last moment to soups or sauces. It can be used plentifully for full enjoyment. Chervil is a very pretty addition to delicate flower arrangements, of particular charm in the old-fashioned nosegays called tussie-mussies (see Glossary, page 163). It is a lovely platter garnish if added at the last moment at table on meat, salad, or vegetables. It flavors cold drinks such as tomato juice cocktail and fruit juices and fruit cups. Chervil is a fine flavoring for omelets, deviled and scrambled eggs, in cottage cheese for hors d'oeuvres and sandwiches, and in any kind of salad—green, vegetable, or potato, for instance. Used bountifully in herb butter, it enhances chicken, fish, and cooked vegetables. It graces hot or cold soups. It may be sprinkled lavishly on chops, fish, and steak, used as a garnish for meat loaf, and is indispensable for Béarnaise Sauce as well as the *fines herbes* combinations. Chervil brings out the best in other herbs and foods with which it is combined, just as some charming people stimulate the others about them.

For centuries chervil was known to be an aid to digestion and was once used in the treatment of gout.

CHIVES

(Allium schoenoprasum)
Hardy perennial

Chives are indeed a kind of Leeks, hot and dry in the
fourth degree, and so under the dominion of Mars.
—NICHOLAS CULPEPER

Chives are among the least "hot and dry" members of the onion
family to which they belong, having a light, delicate, but unmistakable
onion flavor that can be used in most of the ways in which onions
are used. Chives are very popular because plants flourish in many climates, soils, and conditions, being particularly useful in the window
garden. The long, slender, hollow leaves of chives are easily cut with
scissors or with a knife on a board. The pretty flowers, in close round
globes of lavender, look rather like red clover, and they give the herb
garden a touch of color in June and July. These flowers should be
pulled out from the bottom of the stalk before they go to seed, so that
the tough flower stems when dried on the plant will not be mixed
with the green for use in the kitchen; to keep the plant flourishing in
the garden; and to keep the seed from scattering and establishing itself
everywhere around it. The plant makes a pretty edging in the kitchen
garden or even in a flower border.

PLANTING: You may buy chives as a potted plant from herb or
plant suppliers and they may often be found in delicatessens, grocery
stores, and even meat markets. Transplant them immediately into larger
pots for the indoor kitchen garden or put them into the ground outdoors (they like full sun and average garden soil). Chives are also easily
grown from seed, although they grow slowly; or by root divisions.
When you plant seed in the garden, let the little clumps of seedlings
grow closely together, and thin the clumps to eight to twelve inches
apart. Such a planting will increase its size, eventually filling a small
area; in a few years it can be divided. Chives, like tarragon and mint,

Chives

In the Garden

however, are hardy herbaceous perennial plants that must die back to the ground to rest for a period in winter in order to flourish.

HARVESTING: Chives may be cut constantly during the growing season; new leaves will spring up immediately. The plant will even grow back if you cut it almost to the ground for harvesting, although a total shearing weakens the plant somewhat. A boost of plant food will then help it recover. For use in winter, chives may be harvested, cut finely with scissors or a sharp knife, and stored in a plastic carton in the freezer. To use, simply dip a spoon in to loosen and remove the quantity needed, then replace the covered carton in the freezer. This herb is not satisfactorily dried.

VIRTUES: For centuries, chives have been chosen by epicures for mild onion flavoring. They are most amenable, being useful where this onion flavor is desired, but they lack the strong fragrance and onion aftertaste. Chives are therefore socially more acceptable than onions. They are often used in a *fines herbes* combination, or by themselves to give zest to soups, vegetables, cocktail dips, meat, seafood, and egg dishes. Scarcely a green or vegetable salad is not considerably livened both in flavor and appearance by the addition of chives. They are an attractive garnish. Chive butter is useful in seasoning many kinds of sandwiches and hot dishes. In fact, this herb has nearly unlimited uses in the kitchen to make food interesting and lively. If you are skeptical of this claim, try eating Vichyssoise without it; and try potatoes in any form with it.

DILL

(Anethum graveolens)
Hardy annual

It stayeth the hiquet [hiccough] being boiled in
wine, and but smelled unto, being tied in a cloth.
—NICHOLAS CULPEPER

This feathery herb is so abhorred by witches that it is said they will not enter a house where a sprig of it is hung in the doorway. In colonial days in America, dill seeds were one of the herb seeds known as "meetin' seeds," because they were given to children to nibble during long church services to keep them awake. Dill has been known for centuries to have an affinity for cucumbers, demonstrated in the famous dill pickle, by which the herb is chiefly known today. Our grandmothers kept a bed of dill flourishing in a corner of their kitchen gardens for pickles, for medicine, and because they liked its pungent aroma. The dill plant is tall, graceful, lacy, and green with umbrella-like heads (called umbels by the experts) of tiny yellow flowers. The fragrance of dill as a plant is a bit acrid, but the flavor in food is stimulating and pleasantly sharp. Its leaves are often called "dill weed" when found in the markets.

PLANTING: Dill seed may be planted outdoors in spring. Because of its long taproots, it does not transplant well, and so it is best to sow the seeds where the plants are to grow. Thin the plants eight to twelve inches apart; or if the bed is rich, plants may grow closer to-

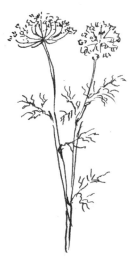

Dill   *In the Garden*

gether, and you may put them six inches apart. The plant shoots up, blooms quickly, and dies when the seeds are ripe, so make succession plantings every three to four weeks if you would like a constant snipping supply for the summer and fall months. Dill seeds itself readily if you leave some plants to do so, and a constant supply is then assured.

HARVESTING: The green foliage of dill can be snipped and used in the kitchen at any time. Use the green leaves and green or dried seeds for pickling. To dry the seeds, harvest the branches when the seeds are well formed and just turning brown. Tie the branches together and prop them in a tall jug, or put them upside down in a paper bag, in a warm, dark, dry place until the seeds have matured. Then shake the seeds into the bag or rub them off into a bowl. You can blow the chaff away and store the seeds in an airtight bottle or can that is kept in a closed cupboard. Dill foliage loses its aroma and flavor when dried, thus freezing of snips of green foliage is recommended, stored in plastic sandwich bags and cartons as already recommended for other herbs. When using, remove the frozen herbs, mince with a sharp knife or Mouli grater, and add to the dish being prepared.

VIRTUES: The flavor of dill has a refreshing sharpness that enhances bland sauces, soups, or vegetables. The chopped leaves provide flavor and attractive color when added to creamed chicken or fish, cream soups, cottage cheese and mayonnaise, potatoes and egg dishes. Tea sandwiches made of cream cheese and chopped dill leaves are a perfect accompaniment to hot or cold plain or herb teas. Dill lemon butter is good on new potatoes. And be sure to try sliced cucumbers with sour cream and fresh dill leaves. Chopped leaves may be sprinkled on tomato juice, split pea soup, cold salmon with mayonnaise, sliced tomatoes, deviled eggs, potato salad, and egg salad sandwiches.

Use the dried seeds for flavoring breads and rolls and cole slaw. Good cooks in New England add a few of the seeds to the water and white wine and stock in which they poach the Fourth of July salmon. Feathery branches of dill are a delightful munching garnish for fish and meat platters, salads, and sandwich trays. And by all means, stay "ye hiquets" with it.

LOVAGE

(*Levisticum officinale*)
Hardy perennial

It hath many long and green stalks of large winged
leaves divided into many parts; the whole plant and
every part of it smelling strong and aromatically,
and is of a hot, sharp biting taste.
—NICHOLAS CULPEPER

Lovage was grown in monastery gardens centuries ago for medicine and flavoring in salads and cooking. It was recommended by the great lexicographer Dr. Samuel Johnson (1700–1784) as a benefit for rheumatism. It was grown in American colonial gardens, and the Shakers grew and sold it for medicine and flavoring just as the monks had done centuries before them. Countrywomen have long considered its use in tea a simple remedy for diverse aches and pains and maladies.

Lovage

In the Garden

   This tall handsome flavorful herb saves many a trip to the market when the cook is faced with a shortage of celery in preparing soup, stew, or a salad calling for it. It has been neglected of late as a kitchen garden plant, and few people know its virtues. But for those who learn to grow and use it, it becomes an indispensable herb. One plant will probably suffice for the average family, and because it is a tall-growing large herb, you may often have room for no more than one. There is a certain kitchen garden where it has grown for years in a corner between house and ell, where it gets morning sun and some drips from the garden faucet—and it is perfectly happy there, furnishing the kitchen with many snippets of fresh celery-tasting leaves and stems, green in summer, dried in winter.

PLANTING: You may grow lovage from seed. The seed germinates best when fresh, and it should thus be sown in the early fall as soon as it ripens. Small plants are available from most herb-supply houses. It is also easily propagated by root division. Lovage likes deep rich soil for its sturdy roots (which have sometimes been used medicinally). It also prefers soil that is cool and damp. This hardy perennial grows from three to six feet tall, depending on growing conditions, and is best used at the back of the garden, against a wall, or in a corner where it has the necessary room.

HARVESTING: If you plant it in good soil and a damp place, you can usually cut lovage back rather severely, two or even three times a year, for harvesting leaves. The leaves dry easily and retain their flavor well if you separate them from the stems and spread them out on screens in a warm, airy, shady room. You can store them whole in a tin and crumble them before use; or crumble them at the time of drying, and store them in tightly capped jars in a dark cupboard. Although the seeds are useful for flavoring, as is celery seed, allowing the plant to go to blossom and seed minimizes the leaf harvest.

Some old-fashioned gardeners like to hill up the soil around the base of the lovage plants, to blanch them and harvest them like celery, but this procedure is tricky and with only one or two plants in the garden it does not seem worth the trouble.

VIRTUES: The flavor of lovage is stronger than that of celery leaves, and it should be used with a lighter touch. Fresh lovage leaves added to soups, stews, casseroles, roasts, and gravy may well provide that extra flavor to make such dishes culinary delights. You may also add the leaves to salads, dressings, marinades, and sauces. Use them finely minced in cheese dishes and to make delicious herb butter. They are particularly valuable in broths and soups, used wherever a touch of celery flavor, or an emphasis of flavor, is wanted. You may candy the stems of lovage for decorating cakes and cookies. Old-timers thought that the scent of the leaves made this herb a good fish bait; and they also made a stimulating lovage cordial.

THE MARJORAMS

Sweet Marjoram (*Majorana hortensis*); half-hardy annual
in the North, perennial in the South.

Wild Marjoram (*Origanum vulgare*), or *Oregano;* hardy perennial.

The whole plant is of a most pleasant sweet smell.
—JOHN GERARD

The early Greeks named the origanums, calling them "joy of the mountains," where they grow abundantly and happily. How lovely it must be to walk across a mountain meadow carpeted with them.

Of the many kinds of marjoram, the two that are of interest in the kitchen garden are sweet marjoram and its cousin wild marjoram, which is better known as (and is hereinafter called) oregano. In cooking, you can interchange the two, although sweet marjoram (as its name suggests) has a sweet and mild flavor, while oregano is more pungent. Their spiciness makes them desirable flavorings for many dishes.

In the garden, sweet marjoram is tender to frost and therefore is treated as an annual in the North. In warm locations of the South, it has perennial qualities. Oregano, on the other hand, is a perennial wherever it is grown, but in the North appreciates a winter mulch of straw or compost around its base. Both of these marjorams are natives of Mediterranean regions. The oregano plants differ considerably in flavor, depending on the area, climate, and perhaps soil in which they are grown. Some have had doubts that plants grown from packets of "oregano" seed were the true wild marjoram of Mediterranean areas. You might prefer getting divisions or cuttings when possible from well-informed herb growers. Lacking this, you can grow sweet marjoram from seed each spring, and you will have an abundance for snippings and harvesting.

PLANTING: You may start sweet marjoram (and oregano) seeds indoors in a warm place and transplant them to the garden when the soil is well warmed. You may also sow the seed directly in the ground, but germination may be slow unless the soil is warm. Marjorams like the sunniest place in the garden and good soil with some sand and lime. After thinning, plants should be six to eight inches apart.

For the indoor garden, take up a sweet marjoram plant from the garden before frost in the fall. Indoors it has a tendency to sprawl, and it does very well in a small hanging basket where its delicate stems can spill over the edges. It *must* have a warm sunny window. Give it an occasional small boost of plant food if you use it constantly for snippings.

HARVESTING: The marjorams have interesting round "knots" for buds, which open into flowers, and the best time to harvest the leaves and flowers is just as the buds start to open. Although you can cut the stems rather drastically for harvesting, leave several inches of stem and some leaves at the base of the plant, and give them a light boost of rich compost (or two tablespoonsful of dried cow manure or one teaspoonful of balanced commercial fertilizer) to help them recover for further growth. Sweet marjoram can be cut again just before frost, and at this time plants should be potted for indoor use in winter. Oregano can usually be harvested twice, possibly three times, during the summer and fall. Just be careful not to cut stems more than two-thirds of their length.

Sweet marjoram and oregano leaves dry well and retain their special fresh flavor when treated as suggested for other herbs (see page 30). They may also be green-frozen in small packets. The leaves when dried emit an even stronger fragrance and flavor than the fresh green leaves, if you have dried them quickly and well. Use them more sparingly than the fresh leaves. If any scent of mustiness develops in drying the leaves, discard them, as is true of any herb.

VIRTUES: You may have to become used to sweet marjoram and oregano before you are sure how much to use without overpowering other flavors in food. Every good cook tastes for perfection, and you will soon become familiar with the herbs' qualities. Sweet marjoram goes well in homemade sausage: fresh leaves if possible; dried leaves if

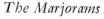

The Marjorams

In the Garden

the fresh are not available. All marjorams have a natural affinity for meats, poultry, and game, and are excellent used in stuffings. Most Americans are now accustomed to the flavor and use of oregano in pizza, and it is time for us to spread the delights of marjorams into everyday dishes such as salads, hamburger, meat loaf, spareribs, tomato dishes of all kinds, broiled steaks, roasts, and chops, and many kinds of hot soups. Marjorams add delightful flavor to egg dishes, and a teaspoon of fresh sweet marjoram on an egg salad sandwich makes it a king's dish. A little fresh marjoram or oregano is also a splendid addition to summer squash, zucchini, and eggplant, lima beans, stuffed mushrooms, vegetable and meat casseroles, grilled cheese and tomato sandwiches; and excellent in *bouquets garnis* for stew, soup, and gravies.

The marjorams have been grown in kitchen gardens for centuries for their warm fragrance and the flavor they add to food. In the Middle Ages they were used as a strewing herb, to disinfect floors and keep them clean and pleasant-smelling. Should there be an unwelcome visiting snake in the kitchen garden, he will soon disappear, for Nicholas Culpeper wrote:

> And thus much for this herb, between which
> and adders, there is a deadly antipathy.

MINT

(*Mentha*)
Hardy perennial

The savor or smell rejoyceth the heart of man, for
which cause they use to strew it in chambers
and places of recreation, pleasure, and repose,
and where feasts and banquets are made.
—JOHN GERARD

All of the many mints have a refreshingly clean fragrance and flavor, and they are familiar herbs to everyone. All members of the mint family have square stems and dainty flowers varying in color from palest lavender to purple. Most mints have rich green leaves with toothed edges and crinkly surfaces. Some mint collectors grow mints with fruity overtones called apple, orange, and pineapple mints; Corsican, lavender, and chartreuse mints; anise, water, and curly mints; pennyroyal; and two cousins, members of the mint family, horsemint and catmint—all fragrant and delightful in their own fashion. For the kitchen garden, however, plant spearmint or peppermint or both because the two varieties are both useful for general cooking and table use. In earlier eras, they were called the "garden mints." In Old London, the flower seller's cry of "Come buy my mint, my fine green mint!" was heard in the streets. Today spearmint has become familiar as a favorite flavoring for chewing gum, peppermint in toothpaste.

PLANTING: Mints do not always grow readily from seed. Beg some rooted pieces of mint from friends, or buy from a plantsman for easy starting. Plant the pieces by laying the runners or roots in shallow trenches or drills, and cover them with well-decayed compost (or soil). They like a bed in a fairly sunny, moist, and well-drained place for best flavor but are not averse to partial shade. In deep shade, they simply grow leggy and do not develop the fine fragrance and taste you would like for kitchen use. Mints need plenty of garden space for their spreading roots, so place them in a bed where they can be.

Mint

In the Garden

controlled or in a place where their wanderings will not matter. You can use wide metal edgings that will contain them well when set deeply into the ground with the top at soil level. You can also use boards, or plant the mints in tubs sunk into the ground.

Mints should not be allowed to go to seed if you want to enjoy the best leaf flavor. There are other reasons, too: the plants will spread even farther afield, and seeding itself may so weaken a plant that it will die. When plants become too thick in the beds, pull them up and replant pieces of the runners to remake the bed. In the fall, cut the whole mint planting to the ground and cover it with well-rotted compost. This is also the time to dig a sturdy plant of mint from its bed to plant in an individual pot for the indoor garden. It would take over a plant box in which other herbs are planted. Like chives and tarragon, this plant will perform better in winter if you allow it to freeze in its pot, buried in the garden to the pot rim, for a month or so of rest before you bring it indoors.

HARVESTING: Harvest mints for drying when the flowers show color and during the morning or late afternoon hours when the leaves have become dry of dew or rain. Handle the leaves gingerly so as not to crush or bruise them, or they will turn black and be of no use. The best method for drying is to snip each leaf carefully from its stem. This helps to hasten the drying time, because the stems retain moisture. Then spread the leaves apart on screens, or frames covered with net, and place them in a dark, dry, airy and warm room at not too high a temperature (below 100° F.). As soon as the leaves are crisply dry, you can store them whole in airtight tins.

VIRTUES: The virtues of mints are so well known, they hardly need listing, but here are some reminders. When combined with apples, mints make a very pretty jelly to serve with meats and game. Mint vinegar and mint sauce should be made with white wine vinegar if possible. Some cooks prefer to use spearmint for jelly and sauces, but you may use peppermint if you do not particularly enjoy the flavor of spearmint. Mints lose their flavor when cooked with vegetables, but sprinkled fresh-green or dried on top of cooked peas or carrots they add a subtle flavor. They are splendid for garnishing fruit salads and desserts, punch and all iced drinks, especially, of course, mint juleps. Applemint or any other mint leaves may be crystallized for garnishing and for nibbling as a confection. You can experiment with mint with surprisingly delicious results—try it on roast beef, for instance, as well as lamb, that old reliable combination. Finely chopped fresh mint can be added to cream cheese and jelly in sandwiches; sprinkled on pea soup or baked squash, chocolate fudge sundaes, fruit compotes, and custards. A couple of handsful in a hot bath are delightful. Orangemint and pineapplemint are favorites in fresh fruit cups and cold fruit beverages. A refreshing and relaxing tea can be made of whole dried or fresh mint leaves, and if you add a touch of honey, you can brew no more enjoyable fireside drink. Spearmint or peppermint tea is said to be good for colds, headaches, and stomachaches.

Following John Gerard's suggestion that "they strew it in chambers and places of recreation, pleasure, and repose," strew some torn leaves of mint on the floors and gather them up in the vacuum cleaner. (You can try some lemon verbena, rosemary, and sage leaves with equal success.) A most delicious scent will fill the air of your rooms.

PARSLEY

(Petroselinum crispum)
Hardy biennial

Parsley is sown in gardens. It flowers in summer.
The roots, leaves and seeds are used. It is a very
good sallad herb.

—NICHOLAS CULPEPER

Parsley has been used over the centuries in so many different ways for so many different things that it surely deserves its high esteem. At one time, it was considered to be one of the most valuable herbs for numerous illnesses, including the "frets" of small children. It was used in victory garlands, for strewing on graves, and for curing baldness. Rubbed on a bee sting, the leaves were expected to relieve the pain. Parsley sweetened the breath and decorated heads, homes, and churches. Better than all these, it was, and is, a flavoring and garnish for good food.

Parsley has no fragrance, only flavor and attractive color. There are two popular kinds: the curled *(Petroselinum crispum)*, which makes the prettiest garnish, and the Italian or flat-leaved *(Petroselinum crispum latifolium)*, which has a softer flavor. Either kind is excellent.

PLANTING: Parsley grows easily from seed, especially when planted in the garden after the ground is well warmed. In cold ground, it takes a long time to germinate, but it will come up eventually; it used to be said that it went to China and back before germinating. Another old-wives' tale warned that it was bad luck to give away parsley plants. No such thing. A gift of parsley in a pot; in a great fresh bunch tied with raffia; or dried and packaged in a jar with a neat label is very good luck indeed, especially to the one who receives it. It was thought that parsley should be sown on Good Friday to prosper, but a gardener living in the North would be more inclined to believe this if Good Friday came in May.

Parsley flourishes in well-composted soil to which a little lime has been added. It revels in high-nitrogen fertilizer (hen dressing, well-decomposed, is excellent), like all green growing things, and likes full sun or partial shade. Plant the seeds "three times their depth"; cover them with fine soil; and thin the plants to stand about four inches apart. You may also have good luck with a parsley border planting not thinned at all. But make the border a good twelve inches wide so that the plants may spread. Parsley is a biennial, and the plants usually live over the winter, especially if you tuck a little dry hay or evergreen clippings under the leafy stems. If you protect them with a slatted box or basket, you can often find a few good leaves even when there is snow on the ground. The plants will flower in the following spring or early summer, and you then should pull them up and reseed the bed. Some people keep the flower stems cut out and say they can keep plants growing for longer than the two years. Old plants, however, become bitter and tough.

If you have room in the garden to give parsley a little bed to itself, you can let it set and drop its seed. It will then establish itself for a continued supply year after year.

For the indoor garden, sow parsley seed in the late summer or early fall and pot the plants when they are quite small. Because of the long taproot, a tall pot or deep box is best for parsley. If your plants do not succeed indoors, this is generally the reason—like teen-age boys, they must have stretching room. Parsley likes a *cool* (but sunny) indoor situation, unlike many other herbs.

HARVESTING: During the growing season, pick the outside leaves of parsley liberally for everyday use. It is possible to dry parsley satisfactorily if you cut the leaves fine with a sharp knife and dry them on trays in a hot oven (375°–400° F.) for a *very few minutes*, until just crisp. They must be carefully watched—burned parsley is of no use whatever! Processed in this way, they retain the lovely green color and much of their flavor. You can also gather small bunches into plastic freezer bags and freeze them, mincing them as you use them. These

A little garden in which to walk.

Plants in pots can be moved out of doors in the spring.

Parsley

In the Garden

bunches wilt when thawed so you cannot use them for decorating a plate, but they have an excellent flavor and make a most satisfactory top garnish for meats or salads. There is a Mouli grater especially made for this job of mincing "persil."

VIRTUES: The flavor of parsley is positive and intense, and a taste for it often must be acquired. It is one of the *fines herbes*, combining well with other herbs. Parsley will in some way grace every meal of the day and every course of the meals (except perhaps desserts): canapés and hors d'oeuvres, soup and fish courses, meats, vegetables and salads, stews, casseroles, cheese dishes, and eggs. Parsley contains calcium and iron, is very rich in vitamins A, B_1, B_2, niacin, and especially vitamin C.

ROSEMARY

(Rosmarinus officinalis)
Tender perennial

They make hedges of it in the gardens of Italy and
England, being a great ornament unto the same.
The floures comfort the heart, and make it merry,
quicken the spirits, and make them more lively.
—JOHN GERARD

Rosemary is an aromatic plant from the Mediterranean countries.
Its scent is said to be wafted across the water to visitors approaching
the shores of those countries by ship. "Dew of the sea" is the meaning
of its Latin name, and there is truly something of the glory of the sea
in its fragrance and flavor, the green and gray of its leaves, the azure
of its flowers. There is also a hint of pine forests, of spices; a clean,
fresh bouquet and taste.

Some of the early uses of rosemary could be revived with charm
today. Brides carried sprigs of rosemary in their bouquets and wound
them with ribbons in garlands for wedding decorations. Sprays were
gilded and given to the wedding guests. In England, rosemary was
used in celebration of the Christmas festival, and sprigs of it were
placed on the altars; pillars were wound with garlands of it and the
floors were strewn with it. A gift of a sprig of rosemary was a symbol
of loving friendship. Sprays were laid on graves. "Rosemary for remembrance" is a universal token. It is, indeed, a sentimental herb.

Rosemary has also been used for many centuries to flavor food. During the Middle Ages it also had many uses in medicine. The graceful
plant has narrow dark green leaves, the edges of which turn under
neatly, like a finely rolled handkerchief hem. Azure flowers bloom at
the axils of the leaves in the spring; tradition says they were always
white until Mary threw her blue robe over a rosemary bush to dry,
and the flowers turned to blue in humble pride at the honor. White-
and pink-flowered varieties may still be found.

Rosemary

In the Garden

PLANTING: Rosemary grows from seed but germinates slowly and uncertainly. Plant the seeds indoors in early spring in a sterile medium such as peat pellets or sphagnum moss. You may, however, find it easier to start plants from cuttings taken from the branches, or from stem layerings. Layering means to peg a branch of a plant into the soil until roots grow at the point that is covered by soil. The new little plant is then cut from the main branch, on the old-plant side of the rooting, and reset into a pot. Stem cuttings also root easily, if you cut them with a little heel of old wood at the bottom of the stem. Strip off all leaves to within about two inches of the top of the stem and sink the stripped length into wet sand, vermiculite, or peat moss. Roots will form in two to three weeks, and you should pot the plants immediately in a mixture of well-decayed compost (or potting soil) and sand. Rosemary likes lime, which you can add in the form of wood ashes, crushed eggshells, or crushed seashells. You may also buy plants that have already been started from herb and plant nurseries.

Rosemary is not winter-hardy. In the cold areas of the country bring it indoors in winter and it will flourish, adding grace, charm, and fragrance to the window garden, to become a real conversation piece as well as a useful adjunct to the kitchen for snippings. In warm areas of the country, you may grow rosemary out of doors year-round successfully, and it will become a large shrub in really warm and sheltered locations. It is often used as a hedge in the southern and western United States, as it was in the early gardens of Italy and England. It becomes a feature of the garden wherever it is grown. You can trim and prune the bushes like the topiary trees of formal gardens, but they are much more charming when left to their own devices. Wintered in the house or in greenhouses, rosemary can be brought out into the garden on a warm spring day, there to stay for the summer.

Rosemary roots must never be allowed to dry out or the plant will die. On the other hand, the roots will not abide standing in water, either. Place the pot on a saucer of pebbles containing a little water and this will keep the air around the plant moist without drowning the roots. Where the air is very dry, spray indoor and outdoor rosemary plants frequently with clear water. A well-potted and regularly watered rosemary will not mind being a little pot-bound, but if its leaves begin to turn yellow, you should probably repot the plant into a larger container, adding new soil.

HARVESTING: You can pinch off the ends of the rosemary branches at any time for use in the kitchen or household. Its aromatic oils are strongest when fresh, and because the plant does so well in the house (or in the garden in the South and Southwest) during the winter, the green leaves are always preferable. Dried or frozen rosemary is not as satisfactory as fresh. If necessary, however, short branches can be clipped two or three times a year from the plants. Strip off the needles and dry them on a screen in a warm, shady dry room or quick-dry them in the oven (see page 31). You may put them through a coffee grinder and store in an airtight container. To freeze, strip the leaves from the stem and store in plastic freezer containers.

VIRTUES: Rosemary as a plant has such virtue in every way, such beauty and dignity, such fragrance and flavor, that it can scarcely be equaled by any other plant.

Leaves of rosemary put into sachets and sprays laid in bureau drawers and linen closets retain their fragrance for a long time and are said to keep moths away. Sprigs tied with ribbons make pretty old-fashioned nosegays. They also make fragrant bookmarks and handkerchief sachets, and a sprig in a party or evening bag is a delight. Sprigs may be used in finger bowls, flower arrangements, and tied on gift packages, or enclosed in letters or cards for a touch of fragrance and "remembrance." It would be lovely to revive the old custom of putting sprigs in brides' bouquets and of giving sprigs to wedding guests. Rosemary plants make charming bonsai, dwarfed plants that are as decorative as flower arrangements.

In the kitchen, rub rosemary leaves on roast beef, roast pork, veal, and chicken to add a rich savor. Insert sprigs into a turkey instead of dressing to give a tantalizingly aromatic flavor to the whole bird. Rosemary with roast lamb is a gourmet's choice; and added to stuffings, the herb enhances both the stuffing and the meat or fish that is stuffed. You can use it in many other ways: added to little meatballs, sausage, casseroles; fresh leaves chopped and put into dumplings, baking-powder biscuits, and pound cake for a delightfully different flavor; in marinades. Brush rosemary butter on grilled fish or chicken and float it on hot soups. Rosemary tea with honey is said to be good for headaches and colds and promotes sociability.

SAGE

(Salvia officinalis)
Hardy perennial

> Jupiter claims this, and bids me tell you, it is
> good for the liver. Sage is of excellent use to help
> memory, warming and quickening the senses.
> —Nicholas Culpeper

In Latin, the word *salvia* means "heal." From Mr. Culpeper's long list of medical uses for sage, the reason for this name becomes apparent. Many old country beliefs and superstitions are connected with this ancient herb. The great English gardener of the seventeenth century, John Evelyn, Esq., in his book *Acetaria: A Difcourfe of Sallets,* said of sage that it was good for the "Head, Memory, Eyes, and all Paralytical Affections. In fhort, 'tis a Plant endu'd with fo many and wonderful Properties as that the affiduous ufe of it is faid to render Men *Immortal.*" Even if it were not endowed with such unusual "properties," it should be in your kitchen garden for its splendid fragrance and flavor in cooking.

Several varieties of sage can be used culinarily, but the common garden sage is readily available in seed or plant form and is the one most frequently used.

Sage is an ornamental plant with pebbly gray-green leaves ("sage green" is the proper description, of course) and long spikes of lavender flowers that bees and hummingbirds love. Sage honey is a delicacy. On a still, muggy day in the kitchen garden, the fragrance of sage permeates the air above all others, except perhaps rosemary. When well-grown and shaped carefully while you snip it for kitchen use, sage is softly pretty, an old-fashioned plant that reminds us of our grandmothers' gardens. An indispensable part of American Thanksgiving dinner, sage goes back farther than that, having deep roots in the history of kitchen gardens.

PLANTING: Sage can be harvested frequently, so two or three plants are usually enough for most families, even though it is an important and frequently used herb. Sage grows easily from seed when planted in spring in the garden. Space the plants from ten to sixteen inches apart. You can also propagate the plants easily from root divisions, from stem cuttings, and by layering the stems. Sage prefers a rather light, even somewhat sandy soil, but grows well in heavy soil if you lighten it with plenty of compost. Apply bone meal occasionally, add a little lime, and give the plants full sun. Sage is a useful and fragrant winter indoor garden plant if you grow it in a sunny window and keep it pinched back to promote bushiness.

HARVESTING: Sage may be picked fresh from the garden all winter, even in the North. Harvest it for drying, however, just before

Sage

In the Garden

the flowers open. Strip the leaves from the stems, place them on a screen, and dry them in a warm shady room. When leaves become crisp, store them whole in an airtight tin, or finely crumble them with your fingers, removing all bits of stem and veins, which become tough and sharp. You should get at least two, perhaps three, cuttings a year from vigorous sage plants, especially if you fertilize them lightly with good compost after each harvest to help them regain strength. Cutting actually helps sage, for it becomes sprawly if you do not keep the stems constantly trimmed.

Sage leaves can be frozen whole for winter use, but it is better to pick them fresh from the garden or the indoor garden, or to use the dried leaves, which retain the characteristic flavor excellently and are somewhat stronger, in fact, than the fresh.

VIRTUES: People who cannot identify the flavor of any other herb will often know sage, and the same might be said of sage plants in the garden. Sage cheese has been made in America for a long time, and it is still available in some areas. For centuries, sage tea has been considered a valuable spring tonic—just pour a cup of boiling water over a handful of crushed or torn leaves and flowers in a teapot, let it steep five to ten minutes, and strain to drink. A touch of honey helps to smooth the flavor. Dried sage has a strong, rather bold, flavor that is best used carefully. This flavor is compatible with game, roast duck and goose, pork, and veal, and is useful in counteracting their richness. This is perhaps why Mr. Culpeper relayed Jupiter's claim that it is good for the liver. The flavor of fresh sage is delicate, not as pungent as the dried. Either is good for turkey or chicken stuffing.

Sage adds flavor to broiled meats and fish, to broiled or scalloped tomatoes, to stews, soups, and casseroles. It is indispensable to good pork sausage and makes a delicious spread when combined with cheese. Crumble a little sage into fish chowders and in broiled lobster or shrimp dressing. Combined with other herbs, sage is a fine addition to a *bouquet garni* for the court bouillon in which you cook shrimps or fish or the liquid you use to make stews and corned beef.

THE SAVORIES

Summer Savory (*Satureia hortensis*); tender annual

Winter Savory (*Satureia montana*); hardy perennial

Keep it dry by you all the year, if you love
yourself and your ease, and it is a hundred pounds
to a penny if you do not: and withal, take notice
that the summer kind is the best.
—NICHOLAS CULPEPER

The savories are so indispensable to good cooking and health that you have a choice of a perennial or an annual variety, each of which has its virtues. Savories have been included in kitchen gardens for medicinal and culinary use for several thousand years, and were planted in American colonial gardens. Both types of savory are strong herbs, to be used with a light touch; both are said to be an aid to digestion; and both have delicious flavor when used with discretion. The summer savory is the more delicate and is recommended by many gourmets, but the winter savory makes a prettier garden plant and does not have

Summer Savory   *In the Garden*

to be replanted every spring. Furthermore, winter savory makes a more satisfactory houseplant in winter than the summer variety, and its tips can be harvested from the outdoor garden all winter if protected in the North by a covering. So here is your choice; it is unlikely that you will need both kinds in a small kitchen garden.

PLANTING: Summer savory grows very quickly and easily from seed planted directly in the garden. Use thinnings in salads or cooking, and space the plants from four to six inches apart. If conditions are to its liking and you let some of the plants go to seed, a bed of summer savory will keep itself going; in a restricted space, however, it is more satisfactory to sow each year. Both savories like good drainage, average light garden soil, and full sun.

Winter savory is an attractive, small, shrubby plant. Grow it from seed planted early in spring indoors, or sow in the ground early in spring when soil is warmed. Its growing requirements are simple, but watch the winter drainage to insure that the plants never stand in water.

Protected by a light mulch of dry hay or evergreen tips, or a box or basket, winter savory will stay green and usable all winter. You can propagate this plant by stem layerings, if you pull branches to the ground, cover them with soil, and leave them over the winter to develop roots. In the spring separate the new plants from the main stems and plant them elsewhere in the garden.

HARVESTING: You can clip summer savory in June or July for drying or freezing. In the fall pull the whole plant out of the ground, cut off the root, and hang the tops in bunches to dry in a warm airy room. Or spread them on screens and turn them every few days until dried. Then strip the leaves from the branches and store them. It oven-dries well; also whole sprigs may be frozen in small plastic bags and placed in freezer cartons.

Harvest winter savory by cutting off branch tips before flowering, and dry them. Crumble and store them when crisp. As suggested before, winter savory can also be snipped fresh from your garden during all but the heaviest weather; and it makes a very good indoor garden plant to use fresh in your house all winter.

VIRTUES: As the old herbalists believed, the savories were valuable as aids in digestion and so they have been cooked for centuries with "beanes, peason and other windie pulses," which in twentieth century English means beans, peas, and other flatulent foods. Their spicy flavor is especially appreciated if you are on a salt-free diet, for the herb's name savory comes from its piquant ability to make food more palatable. Savories are delicious in green and raw vegetable salads; sausage and pork dishes; stews and soups; and cooked vegetables, especially string and other kinds of beans. Casseroles, meat loaves, and small meatballs are given a boost with a bit of savory. Add sprigs of the savories to a *bouquet garni,* and the leaves to *fines herbes.*

Remember that summer savory is lighter and more delicate; winter savory strong and zesty. Both should be used carefully—flavor, taste, and then savor, always, with these herbs.

Bothered by wasp, bee, mosquito, and blackfly bites? It was once believed that rubbing on the leaves of savory would give quick relief.

TARRAGON

(Artemisia dracunculus)
Hardy perennial

Tarragon is not to be eaten alone in sallades, but
joyned with other herbs as Lettuce and such like;
neither do we know what other use this herbe hath.
—JOHN GERARD

Two kinds of tarragon are generally available to us, the "Russian" and the "French," or true, tarragon. Bear in mind that any seeds listed in catalogs will be those of the Russian tarragon, which is not worth growing because it lacks flavor. True tarragon *must* be propagated from root or stem cuttings because it seldom blossoms, and even when it does flower, it never sets seed.

Tarragon is a neat graceful plant with long, narrow, dark green leaves, and it will grow to considerable height if not snipped back for kitchen use. But you will find this temptation too strong to resist, and your kitchen garden tarragon plants will probably be of medium height and bushy. The flavor is sharp and cool, delicate but strong, sweet but tart, with overtones of anise or licorice. The haunting flavor adds to the excitement of using this herb in the kitchen.

PLANTING: You may buy tarragon from herb growers and many nurseries, or beg cuttings from a friend who has a plant he is willing to share. Root cuttings are easily made in early spring. Keep them potted until well rooted, then set the plants into the garden when the ground warms. Tarragon likes a well-drained, sunny location in soil that is light and not too rich. It likes a little lime or wood ashes but little or no fertilizer. When the plant is well established, and branches are six or eight inches high, you can begin to make discreet snippings; this helps keep the plant bushy and neat.

Tarragon lives over the winter more reliably if you tuck little evergreen fir pieces over the roots of the plant after the last cutting and when the soil is frozen. In the spring when you remove the covering, green shoots will spring up again and flourish for cutting all summer.

If you want to have a plant in the winter window garden, pot rooted cuttings of tarragon in the early fall. Sink the pot into the ground until the top dies, and leave it for a rest period of a month or two of freezing or cold weather. Then bring it indoors for the winter. Tarragon does not really relish indoor life because its roots like to spread widely, so put it in a generous pot, give it good drainage without too much watering, and place it in the sun.

Tarragon roots wind among themselves so that they will strangle the plant unless you dig, divide, and reset it every four or five years.

HARVESTING: As with other herbs, you may snip tarragon all during the growing season, whenever you need the leaves for cooking. To harvest it in quantity, make two cuttings, each of two-thirds the length of the branches, during the season. Just before a hard freeze, cut the whole plant to the ground; the top will die anyway after the freeze. This is the time to pot a root cutting for the winter. Tarragon does not dry satisfactorily, but it freezes very well. Sprigs can be put into plastic sandwich bags, sealed, and the bags clipped together or packed flat in a larger plastic carton; remove them as needed in winter. Tarragon may also be preserved in bottles of vinegar; remove the sprigs as needed, rinse them in cold water, and mince them for cooking.

VIRTUES: In spite of Mr. Gerard's complaint that "neither do we know what other use this herbe hath," tarragon's unusual flavor is of great value. It enhances jellied consommé, fish, and chicken. Perhaps it is best known as the flavoring ingredient of tarragon vinegar, which is used for salads and marinades. You may use chopped tarragon with melted butter to add zest to bland vegetables and broiled meats. It is a necessary ingredient of Béarnaise Sauce and is one of the *fines herbes*. You may add it to many sauces and dressings for use in green and seafood salads, and you will find it delicious with mayonnaise on cold salmon. Omelet with chopped tarragon is special, as are scrambled eggs. Put it in the bottom of the cup when shirring eggs, and chopped tarragon will give this Sunday morning treat an extra dimension. It is also wonderful in spring snipped over buttered new potatoes.

Tarragon

In the Garden

Although timid cooks say the use of tarragon should be carefully controlled, others prefer its spicy sharp taste well defined. You will have to decide for yourself how it should be used. Tarragon does not conceal, but helps to bring out, the flavor of the dish to which it is added. It is a wonderful herb to experiment with, a most happy kitchen garden plant, and one that most good cooks hope never to lack.

A favorite tarragon dish is *Poulet à l'estragon* (Chicken with Tarragon). Another favorite is a head of Tom Thumb lettuce on a glass salad plate, with fresh sliced tomatoes or radishes atop, dressed with crumbled Roquefort cheese, one or two tablespoonsful of oil and white wine vinegar dressing, and a dusting of fresh chopped tarragon leaves.

> We may pick a thousand salads ere we light
> on such another herb.
> —WILLIAM SHAKESPEARE (1564–1616),
> *All's Well That Ends Well*

THYME

(Thymus vulgaris)
Hardy perennial

It is originally a native of Italy, but we have it
for the service of the kitchen in every garden.
—NICHOLAS CULPEPER

Thymus vulgaris is only one of many kinds of thyme. It is also sometimes called English thyme, kitchen thyme, garden thyme, or French
thyme. It is the most generally useful of all the varieties.

This herb has been used for many centuries as a disinfectant (and is
still used in some commercial germ-killers). It was believed also to
strengthen the lungs, and to cure gout and hangovers, among many
other conditions. It was once considered a symbol of strength and
courage, and tea made of thyme was drunk to cure shyness.

Thyme plants have a tendency to sprawl unless kept neatly clipped,
but this habit makes them valuable for planting in rock gardens, herb
gardens, and next to the kitchen doorstep. They have abundant tiny
lavender blossoms and tiny leaves. The plants themselves are usually
small and seem to prove the old saying that "good things come in small
packets."

PLANTING: Seed germinates quickly if you plant it directly in the
garden. Thin plants to stand about a foot apart. Thyme likes sun, good
garden soil, a little lime or wood ashes, and a light covering of compost
in the late fall. You can add to an established planting by layering or
stem cuttings, and the plants will also produce self-seedlings.

Thyme does not flourish mightily in the winter window garden, but
if you give it full sunshine, some humidity without too much watering,
and occasional clipping, you will have sprigs for many a special dish,
until spring when you may put such plants back into the garden.

HARVESTING: Thyme can be snipped all during the growing
season as needed. When you are harvesting it for drying cut the plants

Thyme   *In the Garden*

back about two-thirds of their height twice during the season. Do not harvest thyme in quantity after August. The flowers of this herb have flavor and fragrance that are useful in cooking, so the herb should be harvested during the flowering period. After you cut the stems you can dry them in the oven, or spread them out on a screen or tie them in small bunches to dry in a warm room. When thoroughly crisp, the leaves can be stripped and bottled for winter use. Sometimes the stems are sharp and stick into tender fingers, so you may find it wise to wear a pair of clean cloth gloves for this operation, although a better job is done without them.

VIRTUES: Thyme is a strong herb that should be used sparingly for best flavor. It is a valuable bee plant, and thyme honey is redolent of the herb. Thyme honey is especially savored when it is added to any herb tea, or when it is spread on hot biscuits. Include a sprig of thyme in a *bouquet garni* for soups, stews, and sauces or gravies. Pour thyme butter over vegetables, including potatoes, and on meats and fish for broiling to add a warm spicy flavor. It is useful and flavorful in stuffings, egg dishes, and cheese sauce, as well as with roast meats and game. A tiny pinch of thyme on poached, soft-boiled, or coddled eggs is delightful, and chopped fresh leaves sprinkled on hot thick soups are also good. Seafood dishes, especially clam chowder, are benefited by a pinch of thyme—and because this herb has such flavor strength, *"a pinch of thyme"* is a good phrase to remember.

And Four for Good Measure

ANGELICA

(*Angelica archangelica*)
Hardy perennial-biennial

A large and beautiful plant. It is an herb of
the sun in Leo; let it be gathered when he is there,
the Moon applying to his good aspect; let it be
gathered either in his hour, or in the hour of
Jupiter and you may happen to do wonders.
—NICHOLAS CULPEPER

Angelica owes its name to a belief, in the Middle Ages, that it was sent by the angels to resist and cure the dread plague. Not only this virtue, but its fragrance, flavor, and appearance, are of the angels. Although it is not widely grown these days, angelica has unusual and delightful uses, as well as being a handsome garden plant. Thus, if you have room for it, add it "for good measure" to your kitchen garden.

Angelica, unlike most herbs, is a native of the northern European countries, and it is said to grow in the area reaching to the Arctic Circle. Naturally, it prefers a cool situation and grows excellently in

Angelica

In the Garden

partially shady, damp places. Early colonists and travelers to America noted a related species that is native to North America. The plant grows tall, with beautiful green divided leaves. Flowers are white and tiny, in a large composite head on very long stems. Usually it takes the plant two, sometimes three, years to flower. Once you allow a plant to go to seed, it dies; but if you cut out the flower stems before seeds form, the plants will live for several years. This quality makes it a sort of perennial-biennial, if such a thing is possible—two years (or more) to bloom, but living perennially if not permitted to go to seed.

PLANTING: If you want to establish angelica in the garden, it is wise to obtain the seed as soon as possible after it has ripened, in the middle or late summer. When this is impossible, it is better to buy a few plants. In your own garden, if you allow one plant to go to seed the second year, you will have many smaller plants to keep angelica growing in the garden for years. It readily seeds itself. Because the plant grows so tall and needs spreading room for its long stems and large leaves, it likes a place against a wall or building, or in a protected place, even on the north side of buildings in the semishade. It grows under old apple trees where it is allowed to seed itself at will; and it flourishes happily in a damp shady spot under elms and willows.

75

HARVESTING: All parts of angelica—leaves, stems, and roots—could be harvested if you wanted to use it for medicine, as was done in former times. When you are concerned principally with its use for flavor, only the leaves and stems are important.

Leaves of a healthy green color may be harvested at any time during the plant's yearly growth. Cut the stalks close to the ground from the outside of the plant, strip the leaves from the stalk, and dry them in a warm, well-ventilated, dark room to retain color and flavor. When they are dry, you can crush them or leave them in large pieces for storing. The young tender stems are the best to use in cooking, including candying, and you should cut these during the spring growing period.

VIRTUES: The flavor of angelica is unexpectedly sweet and haunting and really cannot be compared to any other taste. Young stems give a lovely flavor to rhubarb sauce; to rhubarb, cherry, and apple pies when diced and mixed with the fruit; and to apple jelly. The stems are hollow between the axils of the leaves, and they make an amusing straw for sipping punch, iced tea, and other beverages. Young tender angelica stems are used for crystallizing and candying, a process better known in France and England than here in America; you can do this easily, as if candying citrus peel. Confectioners decorate fête cakes and delicacies with these sweet apple-green bits of stem.

Angelica tea, made of either the fresh green leaves and stems, or the dried leaves, has an ancient reputation of being good for the digestion and for colic; a syrup of it was believed to help coughs and colds. Try the tea for its flavor's sake, steeping the fresh leaves and stems for eight to ten minutes, unsweetened except for a few drops of honey. Curiously, the leaves alone do not have the typical angelica flavor and taste rather like plain tea, so include a bit of stem in the pot. The stems give custards and puddings a pleasant flavor. Wine can be made of angelica, and it is used among other herbs for flavoring gin, Benedictine, and Chartreuse.

The graceful large leaves of angelica are lovely in flower arrangements, especially when a cool green arrangement of some size is desired in a hallway, beside the fireplace, or in a large room. After a few days the edges of the leaves turn yellow, adding to their beauty and interest.

Once upon a time, angelica was believed to do away with witches. It seems plausible—even today, no witch would countenance being in the same house with a plant called *Angelica archangelica*.

SWEET BAY

(Laurus nobilis)
Tender perennial

> This is so well known, that it needs no
> description; I shall therefore only write the
> virtues thereof, which are many.
> —NICHOLAS CULPEPER

It is true that through the ages men have been familiar with the sweet bay or true laurel. Not only was it an aromatic flavoring for foods, it was a symbol of great honor. Laurel wreaths crowned emperors, kings, scholars, poets, and heroes. The leaves decorated churches, homes, and wedding celebrations. Bay (or laurel) leaves were used for medicine. Today, however, bay is principally useful in cooking. A bay leaf or two flavors many a dish in homes where other herbs are almost unknown.

When you pick bay leaves from your own tree, they are beautifully green, thick, and shiny, with delightful fragrance and flavor. Unfortunately, not everyone can manage a bay tree. It is very tender to frost and must be grown in a tub or other container that can be brought indoors, in northern winters. In the South, in warmer climates, it will grow out of doors all winter if protected from the occasional frosts. There, it sometimes becomes a sizable shrub or tree, an ornament to the garden, as it is when grown in pots in northern gardens.

The sweet bay or true laurel that is used for cooking must not be confused with other plants, especially American laurel, which has poisonous qualities and must *not* be used for seasoning. In cooking, you

Sweet Bay   *In the Garden*

may substitute leaves of seacoast bayberry bushes, although they do not have an intense bay flavor, or use three or four juniper berries instead.

PLANTING: Sweet bay is propagated in this country by taking cuttings from a flourishing plant. It may take a year to establish roots. Small already rooted plants can often be purchased, however, from herb growers and nurseries. If grown in a cold area, put them into pots with good fertile soil made up of well-rotted compost, sand, and if possible some additional well-rotted or dehydrated cow manure. Set them into the garden in their pots, after danger of frost is past in the spring. They will grow best in a partially shady place. At this time, you can clip or trim the tree for shape if you like. Save the leaves for cooking.

When the little tree must be brought indoors—before frost in the fall —place it in a sunny window in a cool room (under 65°) where you can provide some humidity, perhaps by frequent mist sprayings. Bay does well in cool greenhouses in winter. It will also survive in a sunny window in a garage that is not heated but that does not freeze; or in a cool, sunny, cellar window. In the warm South, these precautions are not usually necessary, and you can grow it in the ground. If you are willing to fuss with it, the trouble of growing sweet bay is worth the joy of having green bay leaves to use in the kitchen.

78

HARVESTING: Bay leaves may be picked at almost any time in the growing year for harvesting. Pick them and dry them separately, on a screen in a warm, dry, dark room. Just before they become crisp, press them flat between sheets of muslin or clean white paper under a weight for a few days. Because bay leaves will lose their color, flavor, and scent if exposed to light or stored in paper, they should be stored in glass in a dark cupboard, or in a tightly covered glazed pottery jar, dish, or bowl.

VIRTUES: Bay leaf is one of the indispensable ingredients of a *bouquet garni*. The fresh leaves add a delightful flavor, but they are very strong and pungent and so should be used with great care. Home-dried leaves are even stronger. Break the leaves in half when putting them into the pot, and always remove them before serving the food.

Bay leaf is a classic seasoning for pork roasts, for lamb, and for chicken. It is used in marinades, pâtés, terrines, and in court bouillon for cooking seafood and fish. It is indispensable for cooking corned beef and smoked tongue, and in *bouquets garnis* for soups, stews, and gravies. You can add a leaf or two to the top of a casserole of meat or vegetables while it is baking, removing them before serving. Many vegetables are improved by the addition of a bay leaf during cooking, especially bland ones such as summer squash, zucchini, and eggplant, even artichokes and boiled potatoes.

SALAD BURNET

(*Sanguisorba minor*)
Hardy perennial

Of so chearing and exhilarating a quality, and
so generally commended as (giving it admittance
into all Sallets) 'tis passed into a Proverb.
But a fresh sprig in *Wine*, recommends it
to us as its most genuine Element.
—JOHN EVELYN

Salad Burnet

In the Garden

The proverb of which Mr. Evelyn speaks declared that no salad was good or beautiful without burnet. To some that belief may very well be true, particularly those whose diets do not include cucumbers, the taste of which burnet definitely and delightfully supplies.

This charming green herb is decorative in the garden, where its picot-edged leaves complement the flowers. It is a perennial, but the young leaves are the most flavorful and tender, so treat the plant as a self-seeding annual in order to have a succession of young plants and leaves from year to year. Or keep the plant cut back, and you will encourage the constant new growth of young leaves.

PLANTING: Burnet grows very easily from seed planted in full sun in ordinary-to-poor garden soil. Its flavor and general health are better if the plant is not fertilized. Thin the plants by pinching, so that they stand about eight to twelve inches apart. If you wish to treat the plant as an annual, allow some seed to self-sow in the bed. The old plants will occasionally die off over the winter. Otherwise, the plant will grow as a perennial year after year, furnishing greens from the garden at all times, except in very heavy snow and coldest weather.

HARVESTING: Burnet may be picked green all during its growing season. This is the most satisfactory way of using it, because the flavor of dried or frozen burnet is inferior.

VIRTUES: In salads, burnet is a cool refreshing herb, adding a delicate, fresh, cucumber taste when snipped and tossed with the other greens. It is superb for garnishing all salads. You may float the leaves atop a cup of hot or cold cream soup, to add charm as well as flavor to the dish. You may also cook them *in* hot soups for flavor, particularly cream soups such as asparagus, mushroom, chicken, and celery. Burnet adds a delightful flavor to canned cream soups of all kinds. The leaves can also be chopped and mixed with cream cheese to make a delicious spread.

The use of burnet in claret cup is well known among epicures, as is that of borage, an herb of similar flavor and virtues. It is also an intriguing addition to other light wines and summer drinks, including iced tea and punch. On a hot summer's day, a garnish of two stems of burnet with their fragrant lacy leaves adds flavor and color to tall iced drinks—a pleasant variant, relaxing and cooling. Burnet even *smells* cool.

THE CRESSES

Garden Cress (*Lepidium sativum*); hardy annual

Watercress (*Nasturtium officinale*); hardy perennial

> Those who would live in health may make use
> of this: they may eat the herb as a sallad.
> —NICHOLAS CULPEPER

Although the herbalist John Gerard thought the cresses "nourish little," Mr. Culpeper disagrees, and so do modern herbalists. The cresses, both garden and water, are filled with highly valuable vitamins and minerals. Their flavor is exceedingly good, too, either eaten when used for garnish, or in salads, even in soups. Rocket, another green herb used and grown in ways similar to those suggested for these two cresses, has many ardent fans.

Garden cress, which is sometimes also called upland cress and pepper-grass, is a peppery little plant of the mustard family that grows very quickly from seed planted in pots or flats. Within a few weeks, you can clip it and eat it in salads. It is especially welcome in early spring when a pot of it on your kitchen windowsill furnishes a quick green herb for your cooking pleasure. In the garden, you may sow seeds in succession plantings two weeks apart, for a continual crop of delicate, flavorful green leaves until fall.

Watercress can be grown in little space. For example, in one kitchen garden it grows in a space twelve inches by thirty inches, the dimensions of an old soapstone sink, buried to its rim in a cool half-sunny corner. There is water in this sink, of course, which seeps out slowly through a loosely stoppered drain. There is also a wooden box of compost, sand, and wood ashes, which fills three-fourths of the sink. It is chock full of watercress—delicious, flavorful, vitamin-rich watercress, a relative of the garden cress and of the nasturtium.

PLANTING: Garden cress requires very little attention to perform satisfactorily in the indoor garden, if you plant it in average soil in a pot or pan or flat box. Have you heard of the garden cress gardens that thrive when the seeds are simply spread out on wet blotters or Turkish towels? It might be fun to try this method. In a jelly-roll pan or other flat pan or dish, fold a piece of thick terry toweling (or cut several pieces of blotting paper) to fit the pan. This makes a bed for the seed to thrust its roots into. Pour water into the pan and tilt to soak towel or blotter. Scatter cress seed over the material, cover with plastic film and keep in a cool place (50°–60°). As soon as the seeds sprout and green shoots show, remove film and place pan in a sunny window. Keep seedbed moist at all times. Cut or pull the green shoots at any stage for salad greens, for garnish, and for a fresh tangy nibble of "green stuff."

In the outdoor garden, the seed of garden cress germinates quickly in

Watercress

In the Garden

spring if you sow it in rows or broadcast it in a small area. It needs no thinning except as cut or pulled for the kitchen.

Watercress, too, grows quickly from seed, but its bed must be wet enough for germination, although not so wet that the seed washes away. You need not thin it, and once it is established it will grow on year after year. Its principal needs are fresh water, soil for the roots to grow in, and a little lime or wood ashes to keep the drenched soil sweet. Of course, it grows best along the banks of a freshwater brook or spring. Lacking these, you might use an old sink or a tub, adding water every few days from a garden hose, a dripping faucet, or even a watering can.

HARVESTING: Garden cress should be eaten while very young for best flavor. When it begins to stretch its branches for flowering, the flavor becomes bitter and the cress becomes tough. So harvest young cress in abundance by cutting off the plants with scissors; and keep replanting new seeds for a continual crop. Any garden cress that is allowed to become too old for use in salads makes excellent material for the compost heap, assisting in the decomposition of all the other material.

Watercress, too, is more tender and crisp when quite young, but even when in bud, its flavor is delicious. In the soapstone sink mentioned, the watercress is continually cropped so that it never reaches the flowering stage. Its energy is thus used in producing more leafy stems instead of maturing seed. If you permit it to go to seed, your watercress bed will propagate itself and spread. Watercress is edible until frost sets in late in the fall. In the spring, garden cress planted early will provide greens until the watercress is big enough to use.

Watercress not only grows in kitchen gardens when nurtured according to its special requirements, but it can sometimes be found growing in the wild where free-flowing clean streams or spring water are present. Once started in such a natural bed, watercress often spreads rampantly, even to the extent of choking the streams. It can be gathered from such beds from early spring until late fall in many temperate areas across the country from East to West Coast.

VIRTUES: Garden cress is at its best as an adjunct to green salads and as a pretty, edible garnish. Its spicy sharp flavor is always welcome and well worth a short double row in the kitchen garden, if your space permits and you can make succession plantings.

Watercress contains a great deal of iron, which may have been the reason for its early use as a remedy for "lost color" or anemia. It provides other minerals and vitamins, especially A and C. Its piquant flavor is a boon to green and fruit salads. With homemade white bread and butter, it makes delicious sandwiches. It stays crisp and fresh long enough to be an excellent and handsome garnish for any food. And cream of watercress soup dusted with freshly grated nutmeg can be a gourmet cook's triumph.

And What of All the Others?

There is scarcely any place to stop when one begins to grow and appreciate herbs. There are anise and borage, which someone is sure to want to grow—but tarragon and burnet are similar in virtues. There is caraway, long since escaped from colonial gardens, the seeds of which can be gathered from the wild in late June or July; and there is coriander, which those who make their own curry powder will want to try. There are hyssop and horehound, costmary and comfrey, sorrel and fennel. All have their devotees.

Many herbs have such fragrance that they often demand attention. There is rose geranium, whose lovely deep-cut fragrant leaves impart such delicate flavor to pound and sponge cakes, sugar, and custards, and such fragrance to potpourri and the window garden—plus all its cousins, the leaves of other scented-leaf geraniums, smelling and tasting of lemon, nutmeg, apple, and peppermint, and other sweet or spicy good things.

Surely, someone will say, lavender deserves a place high in the list of herbs. This is true if herbs of varied household use or sentimental value were included, for lavender has been known and beloved and grown for centuries as an herb to be used to scent linens, clothing, potpourris, perfumes, and soaps. But it is only occasionally used for flavoring food, usually in desserts, or in mixtures of sweet herbs.

Without sweet woodruff, there would be no May wine festivals, and it makes a charming and sweetly fragrant ground cover in gardens and woods. Lemon balm and lemon verbena, which add delightfully fresh flavors to tea and summer drinks, have limited use in cooking, and so must be omitted from these pages. Nasturtiums can be grown for brilliant color; for green seeds, stems, and leaves to eat in salads; for flowers, also eaten in salads, and for garnishing beverages and fruit dishes.

All these have their place and their charms and their uses—and many more besides these. But you are choosing plants for a kitchen garden, and the herbs already discussed will be most useful in the kitchen.

A Chart of Herbs for

ANGELICA
Biennial

Tall-growing plant, preferring a cool place, partial shade, rich moist soil.

Leaves and stems are used fresh or dried.

Useful for flavoring; decorative in gardens and flower arrangements.

Candied and used as a confection or as decorations for puddings, cakes, cookies, custard.

Pieces of stem cooked with rhubarb and other tart fruits.

Ingredient of cordials and wines.

Fresh or dried leaves, stalks for tea.

Flavors jams, jellies, chutneys.

Suggested equivalent: 1 teaspoon dried leaves and stems to 1 tablespoon fresh.*

BASIL
Tender annual

Medium-sized plant, preferring full sun, average soil. Plant seeds in warm soil after last frost.

Leaves are used fresh or dried.

All-purpose herb used in soups, chowders, stews, spaghetti and other tomato sauces.

Seafoods and poultry; with beef, veal, lamb, pork.

In vegetables, especially beans, eggplants, parsnips, tomatoes.

In fresh vegetable and seafood salads and salad dressings.

Fruit compotes.

Egg dishes, including omelets, scrambled, soufflés.

Herb butter, herb vinegar.

Suggested equivalent: ½ teaspoon dried to 1 tablespoon fresh.*

"The tomato herb."

SWEET BAY
Tender perennial

Small tree grown from cuttings, preferring full sun or partial shade. It must be brought indoors in winter in cold climates.

Indispensable for *bouquets garnis*.

Fresh or dried leaves—in marinades, soups, stews, chowders, gravies, hot sauces.

Seafoods, pork, lamb, veal, chicken, corned beef, tongue.

Vegetable and meat aspics; bland vegetables, including summer squash, zucchini, eggplant, potatoes.

Meat and fish pies; vegetable and meat casseroles.

Suggested equivalent: ¼ to ½ dried leaf to 1 large fresh leaf.*

*or to taste

Flavor, Fragrance & Fun

SALAD BURNET
Hardy perennial

Medium-sized plant, preferring full sun, average soil.

Fresh leaves best; useful when cucumber flavor is wanted.

Ingredient and garnish for all salads, fresh tomatoes, cold asparagus.

Garnish and flavor for hot or cold cream soups, including asparagus, mushroom, chicken.

In vegetable and seafood aspics, mayonnaise, herb vinegar.

Added to cream cheese for spreads, sandwiches.

Garnish for iced drinks including tea, fruit ades, punches.

"A fresh sprig in Wine."

CHERVIL
Hardy annual

Small lacy plant, preferring a half-shady, cool place.

A *fine herbe*.

Fresh leaves best; used for delicate taste of anise or licorice.

Hollandaise, Béarnaise, mayonnaise, herb vinegar.

All salads, including green, seafood, fruit, vegetable, aspic, potato.

Hot and cold soups.

Tomato or fruit juices, fruit cups.

Mushrooms, cottage cheese, deviled and other egg dishes.

Top garnish for chops, steaks, fish.

Herb butter.

Attractive garnish for many foods.

CHIVES
Hardy perennial

Plant less than 1 foot tall, preferring full sun, average soil. It is an attractive border or accent plant in the garden.

Sometimes used as a *fine herbe*.

Best fresh (may be frozen); used when a mild onion flavor is desired.

Leaves and flowers—excellent garnish for many foods from appetizers to zucchini.

Flavors vegetable and meat casseroles, meat and seafood loaves; peas or beans, potatoes, succotash, eggplant, summer squash.

In green and seafood salads and aspics; hot or cold soups; cocktail dips with cream, cottage cheese, or sour cream.

Egg dishes, including omelets, stuffed eggs.

Baked potatoes with sour cream.

Herb butter.

THE CRESSES

Garden Cress: low-growing *annual*, preferring full sun, average soil.

Watercress: low-growing *perennial*, requiring a bed of sweet soil, constant supply of fresh water.

Best used fresh.

Garnish for all foods—hors d'oeuvres and canapés, soups, meats, seafoods.

Ingredient and garnish for green and fruit salads.

Sandwiches, with cream cheese or herb butter.

With cold sliced tomatoes and cucumbers; in or on tomato and other vegetable or seafood aspics.

Cream of cress soup with dash of nutmeg.

DILL
Hardy annual

Tall-growing plant, preferring full sun, average soil.

Leaves best used fresh (may be frozen or dried); seeds, green or dried.

Leaves and/or seeds flavor fruit, vegetable, and seafood salads and salad dressings.

In cottage cheese, sandwiches.

Soups, especially borsch, cream of tomato and split pea; stews and gravies.

Seafood (especially salmon) and chicken; steaks and chops.

Vegetables, including peas, potatoes, cabbage, cauliflower, stewed tomatoes.

Sprinkled on cold sliced tomatoes, on cucumber and sour cream.

Seeds, especially valuable for bread and rolls, in coleslaw, sauerkraut, pickles.

Court bouillon, herb vinegar.

Dill lemon butter.

Suggested equivalent: 1 teaspoon dried leaves to 1 tablespoon fresh.*

LOVAGE
Hardy perennial

Tall-growing plant, preferring good soil, cool damp places.

Fresh or dried leaves; useful for strong celery flavor.

Vegetable, especially potato, and meat salads, salad dressings, marinades.

Flavors meat or fish sauces and gravies; broth and soups; meat or fish stews and casseroles.

Stuffings for poultry, game, meat.

Vegetable or fish aspics and cheese dishes.

Minced on roast meat, steaks, and chops.

Herb butter.

Stems may be candied for decorating cakes and cookies.

Suggested equivalent: ¼ teaspoon dried to 1 teaspoon fresh.*

*or to taste

MARJORAM, OREGANO

Sweet marjoram: *hardy annual*
Wild marjoram (Oregano):
half-hardy perennial

The marjorams grow one to two feet tall, preferring warm sunny places, average soil.

Often used in *bouquets garnis*.

Versatile herbs; leaves used fresh or dried.

Enhance stuffings, soups, meat and fish stews, gravies and hot sauces.

Seafood, poultry, game.

Sausage, hamburgers, casseroles, meat and fish loaves.

Tomato dishes; spaghetti and pizza.

Many vegetables, including cooked celery, eggplant, potatoes, summer squash, zucchini.

Flavors green, chicken, egg, seafood salads, and their dressings.

Cheese spreads and dips.

Suggested equivalent: ½ teaspoon dried to 1 tablespoon fresh.*

MINT

Hardy perennial

Medium-sized plants, preferring sun or partial shade, good soil.

Fresh leaves best; also used dried.

Peppermint, spearmint, and other flavors used interchangeably.

Classic garnish and seasoning for lamb; roast beef, chops, steaks.

Jellies, vinegar, mint sauce.

Chopped fresh leaves, with green peas, carrots, squash, fruit salads.

Cream cheese and jelly sandwiches.

Pea soup.

Iced drinks, punches, tea.

Fresh as garnish or snipped into chocolate or fruit desserts, custards.

Fresh leaves, crystallized or candied for garnish and confection.

Suggested equivalent: ½ teaspoon dried to 1 tablespoon fresh.*

PARSLEY

Hardy biennial

Small plant, preferring full sun or partial shade, average soil.

A *fine herbe*.

Best fresh; may be frozen or dried.

The most versatile herb, excellent as garnish or ingredient of many foods.

Chopped leaves and sprigs—garnish canapés, hors d'oeuvres.

Meats, seafoods, cheese, and egg dishes.

Stuffings for poultry, game, fish, meat.

Vegetable, meat, and seafood salads and their dressings.

Parsley lemon butter.

Suggested equivalent: 1 teaspoon dried to 1 tablespoon fresh.*

*or to taste

ROSEMARY
Tender perennial

Shrubby plant, preferring full sun, good soil. It must be brought indoors for the winter in the North.

Best used fresh.

Flavors roast beef, pork, lamb, veal; steaks and chops; poultry and game, especially chicken and turkey.

Meat loaves, sausage, casseroles.

Stuffings, soups, stews, gravies, sauces.

Jelly, herb butter, marinades.

Pound cake, biscuits, dumplings.

Rosemary tea with honey.

Use in Christmas decorations and bridal bouquets; may be dried for potpourri and sachets.

"Rosemary for Remembrance."

SAGE
Hardy perennial

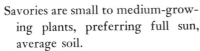

Medium-growing plant, preferring full sun, average soil.

A *bouquet garni* herb.

Leaves are used fresh or dried.

Flavors meat and fish stews, sauces, stuffings, chowders and soups, court bouillon.

Pork sausage, roast pork, pork chops; roast beef, veal, and lamb;

poultry; game and seafoods.

Hot vegetables, including beans, tomatoes, eggplant, summer squash; cold sliced tomatoes.

Chicken salad; cheese dishes, including sauces and spreads.

Sage tea.

Suggested equivalent: ¼ teaspoon dried to 1 teaspoon fresh.*

THE SAVORIES
Summer Savory: *tender annual*
Winter Savory: *hardy perennial*

Savories are small to medium-growing plants, preferring full sun, average soil.

A *bouquet garni* herb.

Summer savory useful fresh, dried, or frozen; winter savory, fresh or dried.

Valuable for salt-free diets.

In cooked vegetables, especially beans and peas.

Meat or fish stuffings, stews, chowders, soups.

Sausage and pork; meat loaf and meatballs; meat casseroles.

Green and fresh vegetable salads, tomato and other aspics, and their dressings.

Barbecue sauce, marinades.

Herb butter.

Suggested equivalents: summer savory, ½ teaspoon dried to 1 tablespoon fresh*; winter savory, ¼ teaspoon dried to 1 teaspoon fresh.*

*or to taste

TARRAGON
Hardy perennial

Medium-sized plant, preferring full sun, average soil, well-drained location. It must be grown from cuttings.

A *fine herbe*, with a taste of anise or licorice.

Leaves best used fresh; may be frozen or preserved in vinegar.

Delicious chopped garnish on canapés, hors d'oeuvres, open-faced sandwiches.

Béarnaise Sauce, marinades.

Green and fresh vegetable salads and salad dressings.

Egg and potato salad.

Seafood or tomato aspics and salads.

Stuffed, shirred, or scrambled eggs.

Hot or cold seafoods, especially salmon.

Poultry, especially chicken and turkey.

Pickles, herb vinegar.

Herb butter.

THYME
Hardy perennial

Low, spreading plants, preferring full sun, average soil.

A *fine herbe* and for *bouquets garnis*.

One of the best herbs for fish and shellfish, including seafood salads and soups.

Meat and vegetable soups, stews, and sauces.

Poultry, game and their stuffings.

Beef, veal, and pork roasts, chops, steaks.

Vegetables, including carrots, beans, peas, potatoes, summer squash.

Green and fresh vegetable salads.

Cottage cheese, custards, egg dishes.

Biscuits, corn bread.

Thyme tea.

Herb butter.

"A pinch of thyme" is a good phrase to remember; a strong herb.

Suggested equivalent: ¼ teaspoon dried (or a pinch) to 1 teaspoon fresh.*

FINES HERBES

Try three or more minced together, to your taste:

Basil / Burnet / Chervil
Chives / Marjoram / Parsley
Rosemary / Tarragon / Thyme

BOUQUETS GARNIS

Try three or more sprigs tied together, to your taste:

Sweet Bay / Chives / Lovage
Marjoram / Parsley / Sage
Savory / Thyme

*or to taste

Chapter 6

The Kitchen Garden Vegetables

Oh, Adam was a gardener, and God
who made him sees
That half a proper gardener's work is
done upon his knees.
—RUDYARD KIPLING

THE BEST WAY TO GET crisp, plump, vitamin-rich, fresh vegetables to the kitchen in their prime is to have your own kitchen garden. With this, everyone should agree.

Yet you may not have the space or time available to grow all those vegetables that it is possible to grow in home gardens. For your kitchen garden, then, choose a few that are easiest to manage in small areas—principally salad crops, and those that are at their best when brought immediately from the garden to kitchen. Some vegetables

take too much space and must be grown in the fields; some demand too much attention (celery, for instance, for which the herb lovage may be substituted). Some require too long a growing season for some sections of the country. Some do not have enough appeal to tempt many gardeners to devote time and space to them. But of the vast choice, some do belong in your kitchen garden, according to your own tastes.

One note as you turn the pages of the seed catalogs—the All-America Selections that are listed there will probably be the most reliable varieties offered.

Eight Favorites

BEETS

(Beta vulgaris)

Beets are among the oldest members of the kitchen garden clan and have been enjoyed as food for more than two thousand years. They are also among the easiest to grow, and are doubly attractive because their young tops make delicious cooked or salad greens. The root is one of the most flavorful and colorful of our table vegetables.

PLANTING: If you have properly prepared your garden soil for other vegetables according to Chapter 3, you should have no trouble growing beets, as they thrive in rich light soil. Do not use fresh manure for any root crop, including beets; compost and leaf mold are excellent, and because beets like a sweet soil, add some wood ashes or lime.

Sow the seed at a depth of three times their thickness early in spring as soon as the ground is ready—this vegetable is hardy and withstands the late spring frosts. The seeds may be planted rather close together and the thinnings used as greens; eventually the plants should be about four inches apart. If you make succession plantings, you can have greens and tender young roots for use all summer and fall. The greens grow rather quickly, but the roots take about two months to reach the most delectable size for cooking.

HARVESTING: It was customary at one time to let beets grow all summer and to harvest them in the fall for winter storage. They are so much sweeter when used young that most gardeners now prefer to harvest them when they are from one to two inches wide and cook them immediately.

USES: When young and tender, beets, as well as the greens, are excellent to blanch and freeze or can for use in the winter. They may be peeled, then sliced or left whole before processing. Beet greens are highly nutritious and a great delicacy if you cook them briefly (just until tender) in the water that clings to the leaves after washing, then serve them with butter and salt, and perhaps a dash of lemon juice or vinegar, or with herb butter. For salads wash them and crisp them in the refrigerator, then toss with other greens, or serve them alone with oil and vinegar dressing. Hard-cooked eggs are a fine garnish for either the cooked beet greens or the salad greens. Fresh herbs such as dill, caraway seed, bay leaf, basil, savory, or mint add interest to fresh cooked beets. You may also pickle ·or glaze them to make a colorful garnish and appetizer.

To cook beets, scrub 1½ pounds of young beets (with root ends and 2 inches of tops attached). Heat 6 cups water, 1 tablespoon vinegar (to preserve color), and 1 teaspoon salt to boiling. Add beets. Cover and heat to boiling; cook 35 to 45 minutes or until tender. Drain and run cold water over beets. Slip off the skins and remove the root ends. You may then reheat the beets in melted butter, either sliced or whole, or dress them as suggested above.

The beet leaves contain most of the vitamins and minerals in the plant—A, B_1, B_2, niacin, and C, iron, and calcium. The roots are also a good source of iron and calcium and contain a small amount of protein. No wonder the beet has been relished for two thousand years.

CARROTS

(*Daucus carota sativa*)

The flavor and other fine qualities of the carrot have been appreciated by kitchen gardeners and epicures for many centuries. In the past it was also used in treatments for wounds, for dropsy, and for the eyes.

PLANTING: A good rich loam or soil that has been liberally treated with well-rotted compost or leaf mold, sand, and plenty of wood ashes or lime is the best for growing carrots, as other vegetables. The soil should be well dug and raked clean of such obstructions as clods, stones, and other bulky materials that might produce deformed roots.

You may plant the seeds very early and rather thickly in a wide shallow trench and press them in with a board. As the plants grow, thin out and eat the tiny new—little-finger size—carrots. They are sweet and delicious raw or cooked and served with melted butter. If you prefer larger carrots, thin them to about two inches apart. Succession plantings may be made for spring, early summer, and fall growing, but carrots do not relish hot dry weather. To help repel any insects that may attack carrots (and beets) grow members of the onion family or strong herbs near them.

HARVESTING: Carrots withstand light fall frosts, but you should pull them before the ground freezes. They may be stored for a reasonable time in the refrigerator, but do not store them with apples either in the refrigerator or vegetable bin, because their flavor is noticeably changed if you do. You may top them and bury them in a box of sand in a cool cellar for winter use, or pull them when they are young and process them for the freezer, that is, blanch in boiling water and quick-freeze them.

USES: Carrots are rich in vitamin A, and they also contain B_1, B_2, and C, calcium, and iron. Small young carrots do not have to be peeled or scraped; scrubbing is all they need. Blender-made carrot juice contains all the valuable vitamins and minerals of the vegetable. Carrots harmonize well with peas in the kitchen; and you might like to use ginger, grated orange peel, or various herbs for a slight change in flavor. They are delicious used raw as appetizers, with a cottage cheese and herb dip, or freshly grated in salads with herbs and greens.

To prepare carrots for cooking, scrub young carrots well; scrape large carrots. Remove ends. Leave carrots whole, cut lengthwise into strips, or crosswise into half-inch slices. Cook covered in one inch of boiling salted water (½ teaspoon of salt to 1 cup of water) until tender. Young carrots take little time—12 to 15 minutes—to cook to the tender stage. Whole carrots (depending on size) are usually tender in about 25 minutes; lengthwise strips, about 18 to 20 minutes; crosswise slices, about 12 to 15 minutes. Carrots may also be shredded and cooked in boiling salted water for about 5 minutes.

The pretty foliage of carrots makes a nice border for a garden walk, especially when you alternate young lettuce plants with them. As you harvest the plants, you can sow new seed for an attractive succession planting.

CUCUMBERS

(*Cucumis sativus*)

One of the oldest of our popular vegetables, cucumber has been relished for over three thousand years. "A lodge in a garden of cucumbers" was mentioned by Isaiah; the Asians, Greeks, and Egyptians knew and enjoyed them.

PLANTING: Cucumbers grow best in richly manured or composted light soil. Although they do not require full all-day sun, they do require plenty of moisture, because they are about 96 percent water. They may be trained over low supports, trellises, or walls and fences; they make a very good cover for compost heaps. You may also grow them easily in large wooden boxes or bushel baskets, if you give them plenty of water and good drainage, as well as in "hills" (see Glossary, page 162) in the garden.

For an early start, plant the seeds in peat pots or in splint or paper strawberry baskets if available; use three or four seeds to a pot, eight or ten to a strawberry basket. You may then set them directly into the garden spot you have chosen, after all danger of frost has passed, pot or basket and all. When seedlings contain six leaves, thin them by cutting off at the ground level with a knife or sharp pruners all but four seedlings to a planting. Or sow the seeds directly into the garden, eight or ten seeds to a planting, thinned to four. When the remaining plants have developed well, nip off the very center point of each plant to encourage compact growing; they should not otherwise be trimmed.

To protect the fruits and to help retain moisture in the soil, you may place hay or straw around the plants to keep them clean, cool, and growing happily.

HARVESTING: As the fruits become shapely and green, they should be picked, for ripening fruit decreases the yield of the vines. The best time to pick them for salads is when the fruit is rich dark green, well developed, and full of moisture. If the fruit appears shriveled or the vines seem wilted they are not getting enough water. Cucumbers are extremely sensitive to frost, both in spring and fall. You should protect them from it by covering them at night with light blankets or sheets, burlap, or other materials. Remove the coverings the following morning.

USES: Fresh crisp cucumbers have an affinity for salmon, and they are incomparable in salads. Try to find some room for them to grow in, even if they have to clamber over the terrace railing or the front-door trellis. You will find them excellent sandwich material and good as an hors d'oeuvre, peeled and cut in fingers or slices. The old-fashioned way of serving home-grown cucumbers—icy cold, unpeeled, scored lengthwise with a sharp fork, and thinly sliced, then dressed with light vinegar, salt, pepper, and a touch of herbs—is still popular (dill is particularly delightful). Cucumbers are also delicious when pickled, as good cooks have known for centuries; and you may use them in casseroles; stuffed and baked; or cut in quarter-inch slices and cooked in boiling salted water until tender (about 5 minutes) and served with butter, herb butter, or cream sauce. Shredded cucumbers cooked briefly in white sauce dress any poached fish. Cold cucumber soup is a summer delight with a fresh herb garnish.

Cucumbers have long been used as a beauty preparation by ladies wishing for white skin and pretty complexions, today as yesterday. The early herbalist Nicholas Culpeper recommended them for use to "cleanse the passages," but probably plenty of pure water would have been equally good for this purpose.

LETTUCE
(*Lactuca sativa*)

By all odds our most important salad green, lettuce is very easy to grow. You can keep a constant supply growing in the kitchen garden from early spring until after the snow flies by succession plantings. Transplant the seedlings to any empty space in the garden, and in the late fall cover small beds with storm sash or plastic frames when heavy frost and snow threaten. There may even be fresh garden lettuce for Christmas dinner.

PLANTING: Two principal types, the loose-leafed and the head, can be grown at home, with a number of varieties of each. For the kitchen gardener, the loose-leafed are satisfactory because they are not so fussy to grow. Their flavor is as good as that of head lettuce. Most of these types will grow a new top from the root if you cut the first top with a sharp knife just above the base of the leaves—this may even happen to plants trimmed by cutworms or woodchucks!

Generally, lettuce will grow well in any good light garden soil. In the North it likes a "warm" mostly sunny spot; in areas where summers are very hot, a damp and "cool" situation is desirable. Some types tend to go to seed quickly (this is called "bolting") if grown in very hot locations. For successful lettuce, enrich the ground with well-rotted manure or compost, and add some lime or wood ashes. Start the seed indoors in flats or put it directly into the garden in early spring as soon as the soil is in good friable condition. Succession sowings will insure a constant supply of plants. Lettuce seed sprouts very quickly. You may plant it in rows, or broadcast the seed in a bed; either way, transplant the thinnings or use them in salads. For larger plants, thin the lettuces to six to twelve inches apart, depending on the size of the variety.

For clean lettuce, put a mulch of clean straw, hay, or dried grass clippings on the ground to prevent garden soil from splashing onto the leaves during watering or rain. This will also reduce your weeding activities. Slugs and cutworms love lettuce (pages 25–26) and an occasional little green worm may be found feasting on its fresh crispness, but if you plant a little extra seed to compensate for losses, and watch out for the pests, you will make up for small damage.

HARVESTING: It is best to pick lettuce early in the morning. Wash it in cold water, being careful not to bruise the tender leaves, and then crisp it in the refrigerator until needed at table.

USES: Fresh green lettuce leaves from the garden contain vitamins A, B₁, and C, and small amounts of protein and sugar. Oak-leaf lettuce adds rich color to salads; Salad Bowl is handsome, with frilly light green leaves. Buttercrunch is crisp, rich, and juicy, possibly the best leafy variety, and it makes an attractive individual green-salad serving when picked full-blown. Tom Thumb is perfect for small areas and windowsill gardens; it is also worthwhile in the kitchen garden, for its very small crisp green heads make easy-to-serve individual salads and garnishes.

Lettuce has affinities, it is said, and in the garden it grows especially well with herbs. In salads, it is enhanced by the companionship of many herbs; by such old favorite vegetables as cucumbers, radishes, onions, and tomatoes; and by fruits.

Sometimes people "wilt" lettuce by dousing it with hot salt pork or bacon fat, but its fresh flavor is lost in this way. Better to combine it with many good kitchen garden friends in salads, sandwiches, and as an edible garnish.

THE ONION FAMILY
(*Allium*)

Onions are a very important vegetable family, truly as old as the hills. They are referred to in the Bible and pictured on early Egyptian monuments. Historically, they have been grown for medicine as well as for flavoring. Some member of the family may be grown, at some part of the year, in any area of our country that has the required soil and moisture. The onions are universally used for seasoning, cooked or raw, and for pickling. They are propagated and grown from seed; or from bulbs or parts of bulbs that split into sections and are planted in the ground; and sometimes from bulbs that grow at the top of the plant.

PLANTING: In general, the soil for growing onions should be well drained, rich, and thoroughly prepared. Commercial growers pay the utmost attention to preparation of the soil for onions, cultivating it deeply, enriching it highly, and liming it generously. Someone has suggested that the soil for growing onions should be so pulverized that it can be put through a fine screen, and that it should contain quantities of rich well-decayed manure, compost or leaf mold, and lime or wood ashes. Plantings must be kept free of all weeds, and the land must have good drainage. With all these "musts," it may seem that it is too difficult to grow onions well, but in the home garden their requirements are not so frightening. Rich well-tilled garden soil suits most members of the family well, and keeping them free of weeds is not more essential to onions than to any other kitchen garden plant. Members of this family take up little space in the garden and are well worth growing.

Onions require all three of the chief elements of plant food, nitrogen, phosphate, and potash, and many gardeners like to side-dress the rows with commercial fertilizer. Organic gardeners believe that a well-composted soil produces onions of equal quality and size (if not better) without commercial products.

You may grow onions from seed planted in the garden, but it is generally more satisfactory if you buy "sets," so that the growing time is shortened. These sets are tiny onions that you may get in the market or from seedsmen. Plant them three inches deep, very close together, pointed ends up, early in the spring; in the South they are often planted in the late fall. When the plants are three or four inches tall, thin every other one and use the thinnings as young salad seasoners. An old adage directs gardeners to thin again "when the plants are the thickness of the finger," and these thinnings can be used as spring onions (sometimes called green onions or scallions), raw as appetizers and in salads.

HARVESTING: Onions show their ripeness when the tops turn yellow and bend over. If they do not all yellow at once, bend over the remaining tops by hand; this stops their growing. When the tops are dead, pull the onions and lay out under cover on a garage or shed or porch floor to "cure." Or braid the tops and hang the onions in a warm room to dry for several days. Once dried, you may store them for months in this way, in a cool place.

USES: Members of the onion family are endowed with vitamin C and contain small amounts of sulfur and calcium. The tops of little green onions contain vitamin A as well.

One of the popular members of the family, the Egyptian onion (*Allium cepa viviperum*), also called tree onion, Canada onion, and top onion, is a true perennial. It is an easy plant for the kitchen garden, for it can be left in place year after year, to be harvested as you need it in the kitchen. It has a mild true onion flavor. The bulbils that grow at the tops of the stems may be peeled and used for seasoning, or you may plant them to propagate more plants. Slice the hollow leaves or stems into sections, split and stuff them with cream or cottage cheese for appetizers or salad garnish, or slice them thinly for salads, especially green and potato salads. You can use the bases of the stems in cooking like leeks. When the stems of Egyptian onions bend over, the little bulbils take root in the ground and increase the planting without help. You may buy these bulbils from some herb suppliers and seedsmen.

Leeks (*Allium porrum*) for cooking are difficult to find on the market in this country, although they are plentifully grown and used in Europe. Sow the seed early in spring and thin the plants to six inches apart. Some growers like to transplant the seedlings into deep trenches and gradually fill the trench in with soil. This produces a long, white, fleshy, thick stem that is tender and delicious. You may have equal success hilling the soil up around the growing plants and mulching to create the bleached stems. The latter method is probably preferable for the small gardener. You may harvest leeks in the fall, or leave them in the ground and dig them out at any time during the winter if the ground is not frozen too solidly. They thaw out well and do not rot in the ground. Dig out the remainder of the crop as soon as frozen ground thaws sufficiently in late winter, before the leeks begin to toughen.

Leeks are better cooked than raw, and you will find them an excellent flavoring in puréed vegetable soups (particularly Vichyssoise), and with lamb, chicken, or rabbit in stews. Leeks are delicious boiled and served with lemon butter, herbed butter, or Sauce Vinaigrette. Basil, rosemary, thyme, and ginger are good seasonings for cooked leeks. Chilled after cooking, leeks may also be served in salads with tart herb dressing.

To prepare leeks for cooking, remove the green tops to within two inches of the white part. Peel the remaining outside white stem and split with a sharp knife, washing out any sand or dirt. To cook, heat to boiling about one inch of water to which is added ½ teaspoon of salt per cup of water. Add leeks. Cover and heat to boiling; cook 12 to 15 minutes or until tender. Drain.

Why doesn't everyone grow garlic (*Allium sativum*)? This sturdy pungent member of the onion family is extremely simple to grow. You need only buy a large firm garlic bulb at the grocer's, separate the cloves, and plant them early, three inches deep, three inches apart. They will grow like other onions until the tops yellow and fall over. Then you pull them, dry them, and keep them for winter use in the kitchen. You may also plant the cloves in a windowsill pot for snippings, used like chives. Garlic may be pulled when ripe, cleaned, dried, and braided to hang in the kitchen for use and decoration.

Shallots (*Allium ascalonicum*) are a mild sweet member of the onion family raised from sections or cloves like garlic. Plant the cloves four or five inches apart just below the surface of the soil. Pull them when the tops die down, and dry them like onions and garlic. After drying, you can keep them in a basket or net bag in the kitchen where they will be handy.

Shallots require a minimum of attention and cultivation in the kitchen garden. It is a wonder that they are so seldom found in the markets, for their flavor is very desirable in preparing many dishes. One clove produces many bulbs, which are divided into more cloves. They seldom spoil, although of course after a long time they will dry out. In the spring, you may plant any that are left over in the kitchen basket out in the garden, and you might do well to plant a few extras to provide cloves for the next year's planting. Shallots can now be bought from some seedsmen or from purveyors of health or gourmet foods, but they *should* be commonly available.

Shallots may be used wherever you want a mild onion flavor and fragrance, especially in salads, soups, or stews, in cooking chicken, some types of fish, and in casseroles with other vegetables.

Another member of the onion family that belongs in every kitchen garden, indoors or out, is chives, which are treated as herbs (see page 44).

PEPPERS

(*Capsicum frutescens*)

Peppers, whether sweet or hot, are a plant for the sun and the South. They are native plants in South America and have been used for centuries for flavoring and as medicine for colic, toothache, and such.

PLANTING: You can easily grow peppers in the North if you start the seed indoors about two months before the last frost date. Transplant the seedlings to the garden when the ground is well warmed. You may also buy plants from local growers, all ready to put into the garden when frost-safe. New hybrid varieties yield fine, disease-resistant plants bearing fruits of excellent flavor and size.

All peppers like good rich garden soil. Plants should be spaced at least a foot apart. Some varieties bear so heavily that staking to support the plants is suggested. Some gardeners like to harden off peppers after planting by putting paper caps (usually called Hot-Kaps in garden catalogs) over them to keep them snug and warm until they are adjusted to outdoor life. They are extremely tender to frost, but once summer with its warm sunshine arrives, they flourish. They are not much bothered by insects.

HARVESTING: Sweet pepper bears large bell-shaped glossy green fruits of a mild flavor. As the fruits ripen on the vine, they turn red and add a dash of color to the garden, as well as to salads, vegetables, and pickles. Four plants would probably be enough for the average family. While fresh green peppers do not keep well for storage, they may be fresh-frozen. Seeds and inner membranes may be irritating and should always be removed before using peppers for food.

Hot peppers are long, narrow, and bright red. Depending upon your interest in this hot, peppery, pungent vegetable, two to four plants should be sufficient, for a little goes a long way. For winter use, you can string the hot peppers together and dry them by hanging in a hot dry room, attic, or shed for several weeks. In Spain, Mexico, Morocco, India, and other countries, the strung peppers are sun-cured and dried. They are a very important addition to the cookery of such countries.

USES: Peppers are high in vitamins A, B$_2$, and especially C and contain other food value as well. They are a handsome kitchen garden plant as well as a useful vegetable in the kitchen.

Sweet green peppers may be used as an ingredient or edible garnish for all kinds of salad and cold plates; they may be stuffed with herbed cottage cheese and sliced crosswise; they may be parboiled, stuffed with meats, seafood, or vegetables, and crumbs and baked whole; they may be chopped and added to salads, casseroles, and vegetable dishes (remembering to remove seeds and inner membranes). Chopped green or red-ripe, they add gay color to a dish of mixed pickles, corn relish, or corn-off-the-cob.

Hot peppers are used to provide a sharp biting flavor for hot sauces and soups, for frying or canning, and for pickling. When thoroughly dry, they may be hung in the kitchen for use, a pretty decoration. They may also be chopped into flakes, or ground in a mortar to a powder to make a cayenne for spicing. Barbecue sauces usually contain some of this seasoning.

Peppers can be grown very successfully in pots outdoors; or in a warm sunny window indoors, making fine houseplants.

RADISH

(*Raphanus sativus*)

The radish has so long a history that someone once wrote a whole book about it, and early records in China, Egypt, Greece, and Rome demonstrate its popularity as a salad vegetable. John Evelyn, who in

*Little gardens may be grown on a windowsill
or in a window box.*

*A kitchen garden in a variety of containers offers
a generous bounty of sweet, tender herbs.*

1699 wrote the delightful treatise on gardening and cookery called *Acetaria: A Difcourfe of Sallets* (sic, "salads"), in very picturesque wording asserted that the radish "affords a very grateful mordacity and fufficiently attempers the cooler ingredients" (of salads). It is indeed so.

PLANTING AND HARVESTING: Radishes are generally of two kinds—the red globe or top-shaped, and the long white icicle-shaped varieties. Favorites are the round red Cherry Belle and the white-tipped red Sparkler, but adventuresome radish fanciers will find other kinds equally good.

Radishes must be quickly grown in cool weather to be at their sweet, crisp best; in hot weather they become pithy and bitter. They like soil of fine tilth (a lovely country-sounding word that means finely crumbled), as is true of any root vegetable, so that the root will not be deformed. Rake the soil fine, then make a shallow trench about two inches wide; scatter the seed into the trench, cover it lightly and firm the soil. If you have an unexpectedly empty area in some corner of the garden, broadcast a little radish seed, firm the ground, and water. Radishes will succeed in almost any nook in the flower, herb, or kitchen garden. Because they sprout and grow so quickly, they come and go in no time, and so are excellent for succession sowings during the cool spring and early summer, and again in the fall, even in the winter in some areas. Radishes are frost-hardy and can be among the earliest and latest seeds sown.

Make only short rows or plantings of radishes at any one time, at intervals of ten days or two weeks during suitably cool weather. A large planting will be wasted unless your family really dotes on radishes. They cannot be stored and must be eaten raw when fresh, before they become large and bitter.

Radishes are sometimes troubled by an insect that eats into the roots, but if you rake a heavy dressing of wood ashes into the soil before planting it will help eliminate this pest. It would be interesting to know if a previous planting of marigolds in the ground where radishes are grown would eliminate this root weevil as it does the nematode.

USES: Although radishes contain minute quantities of vitamins, they do not provide much food value. They are appetizing, however, as crisp bright additions to salads and as a garnish. To make the popular radish "roses," peel the sides like petals downward almost to the base with a sharp knife; then set the radishes into ice water so that the "petals" thus produced will curl a little. Perhaps you like to dip the tip of the radish into salt for eating—you will find them most delicious if you scrub them clean, cut the tops off to within a half inch or so of the radish to supply a little handle, and cut the taproot off completely. To make a refreshing sandwich, slice radishes thin and dress them with salt or a little mayonnaise. For the hors d'oeuvre tray, halve radishes and top each half with herbed cream cheese.

There is a winter radish that grows and may be stored and cooked like turnips, but few seed catalogs list them these days, and in a small garden and average kitchen, you are unlikely to miss them.

TOMATO

(*Lycopersicon esculentum*)

Tomatoes made the arduous journey from the warm areas of the newly discovered Americas to Europe, and they did not come back to us until the end of the eighteenth century, although they had been much relished in warm countries of Europe in the interim. Northern Europeans and Americans thought them quite poisonous, and our ancestors here did not use them freely until Thomas Jefferson and a few other intrepid gardeners were persuaded of their value for the table.

Today, however, the home-grown tomato is surely one of the favorite vegetables of most American families.

You may have tomatoes for all tastes: red, tangerine, yellow, white, and pink; giant, large, small, and tiny; round, ribbed, and elongated; acid-free (or nearly so); early, middle, and late ripening; and even a special kind for growing in containers on the patio, appropriately named Patio. Many hybrid varieties are remarkably resistant to disease; most seed catalogs are careful to point out the best of these.

PLANTING: If you would like to have plenty of a favorite variety of tomato in the northern kitchen garden, it is wise, and can be fun, to start the seed indoors in a sunny window six weeks to two months ahead of safe-planting time. Plants may often be ordered ahead or bought from local growers. If you do buy them, choose plants about ten to twelve inches tall, in individual pots, for the quickest harvesting. Because tomatoes are slow to reach maturity of fruit, seeds do need to be planted early in any part of the country, but in the South, they may be put directly into the ground.

When sown in pots, strawberry baskets, flats, or compressed peat wafers, tomato seed sprouts quickly and easily. If seedlings grow fast, you may transplant them once into larger pots and then set them into the garden after all danger of frost is past. You may cover them with Hot-Kaps to help harden them off and keep them warm. If the plants have become tall and leggy in their pots, you can plant them in a deep narrow trench with about six inches of leafy tops above the soil. Many roots will grow from the submerged stems and the plants will be sturdier and more vigorous for this treatment.

Tomatoes are not particularly fussy about soil so long as it is suitable for other vegetables, but they like plenty of water, and in dry seasons or in dry areas extra watering may be necessary. Watering with manure tea once a week also gives them vigor and strength and encourages them to produce more and larger fruits.

Cutworms have a predilection for young tomato plants. To discourage them, surround the newly set plants with stiff paper collars (paper cups may be used for this purpose, with the bottoms cut out) when putting them into the ground; then put a halo of wood ashes outside of the collar to further discourage these hungry little pests. Occasionally you may find that leaves of a plant are being eaten, and black droppings may be noticed on the plant. This usually means that a pleasant butterfly has become a green tomato hornworm (he wears a tiny "horn" at his rear) and is hungrily devouring the plant. He may completely destroy it in a short time if you do not remove him. The least troublesome way is to snip off the entire leaf on which he is resting and drop leaf and all into a can containing kerosene, rubbing alcohol, or even beer. The hornworm is ugly but he does not harm people, so you do not need to be squeamish or afraid of him.

Tomatoes enjoy being tied to a stake. A number of them in a row at the end of a terrace, beside the outdoor cooking area, or in other convenient locations, make a pleasant and colorful "fence," or accent. If you stake your plants, you must put the supports into the ground at the time you set in the plants, and the stakes must be sturdy. Nothing is so discouraging as to find after a storm that a heavily laden tomato plant has pulled over its stake and had its branches broken. Supports should be six or seven feet long and pounded deeply into the ground; tie the plant as it grows, four or five times during the season, with soft ties, preferably made of cloth (old nylon stockings are fine for this purpose). Most gardeners like to prune tomatoes to a single stem or at most two main stems, pinching off the suckers that grow at the axil between branch and stem. If you really wish to display your gardening prowess, put in very tall stakes and encourage the plants to grow upward just for the fun of it.

Tomatoes also enjoy sprawling on the ground without pruning, providing you mulch them well with straw or grass to keep the fruits clean and the soil underneath moist. This method of growing takes more room than staking, but such plants are easily covered for protection against frost in the fall. It may be the lazy gardener's way of growing tomatoes, but it is often successful. You can also train plants to grow over low walls, trellises, or wooden braces. Some varieties are particularly suitable for growing in containers (see Little Gardens), and a hanging basket of Tiny Tims in a warm sunny window in winter can provide salad garnish for months. A hormone preparation is now marketed by seedsmen and nurseries that is sprayed on the plants when they are in blossom to increase the set of blossoms, to produce better, larger, and more fruits, and to ripen the fruits earlier. The product has been tested by the United States Department of Agriculture. It is sold by the bottle to be mixed with water, and also in aerosol cans for easy application. This product is used by some commercial growers as well as home gardeners.

HARVESTING: If you cover plants in the fall when frost threatens, perhaps using old sheets or light blankets, you may sometimes stretch the producing season by as much as a month. Country people often say that the full moon of an autumn month may bring a frost, and then the weather warms again until the next full moon. It is often true. When these first cold nights arrive, pinch off all remaining blossoms and the top of the plant, which has the effect of putting all growing vigor into the fruit remaining on the vine. When a hard freeze is predicted, pick all ripe and nearly ripe fruits and keep them in a cool place. To use the larger green fruits, make piccallili (see page 157), chutney, or green tomato pickle, or fry them. The old-fashioned way of pulling up the vines and hanging them upside down in a shed or basement—dirt, roots, and all—is messy. The sun and its warmth give tomatoes their marvelous flavor, and fruit that is ripened thus artificially seems tasteless after you have enjoyed the fully sun-ripened, juicy, flavorful fruit all summer and fall.

USES: Nothing in the gardening world is so great as the first sun-ripened tomato from the kitchen garden. It is rich in vitamins A, B_1, B_2, and C. Home-canned tomatoes are marvelous substitutes for the fresh in winter. The good qualities of tomatoes are less destroyed by canning than those of any other fruit or vegetable, and the canned product is essential for winter use in making soups, stews, vegetable and meat casseroles. Homemade juice, catsup, soup, chili sauce, chutney, and other pickles may be canned using any extra tomatoes you cannot eat fresh, and they are all very easy to prepare as well as economical. You will find literally hundreds of ways to use either fresh or canned tomatoes in the kitchen. The acid in this vegetable makes it especially suitable to the cold-pack method of canning, and one bushel of firm ripe tomatoes fills about fifteen to twenty quart jars.

Tomatoes have a special liking for parsley, basil, chervil, thyme, marjoram (including oregano) and sage, as well as salad vegetables, summer squash, and onions. Tomatoes and cheese are also good companions, especially in pizzas, pastas, and casseroles.

Elbowroom Vegetables

Even Martha Washington did not have sufficient room for some vegetables in her plenteous kitchen garden at Mount Vernon. These had to be relegated to outlying spaces or fields, to be tended by her husband's farmers. True, she often had short rows of peas, or beans, and one or two plants of rhubarb. But to raise enough for her establishment—or any growing family—field rows are more efficient and productive. Nevertheless, some kitchen gardeners put in a few hills of green beans, which are allowed to climb on tall poles; or peas, which may be trained on fishnet at the back of the garden to supply enough for the annual Fourth of July feasting on new peas. A squash vine may be planted on the wall, or runner or pole beans may be put on strings around the kitchen window instead of morning glories. If it pleases you and you have a corner for planting, you may include one or more of the following choice vegetables in the kitchen garden, but remember that they need elbowroom.

Two perennials, asparagus and rhubarb, grow on year after year. They are handsome plants, sufficiently so that they will fit into any flower garden or herbaceous border if you have no room anywhere else. They must be located where their roots will be undisturbed during the years; and both require very rich soils for best performance. But they are worth every inch of space they occupy.

Three other vegetables, beans, corn, and peas, are popular and delicious when grown at home, and their cultivation is also briefly described. You will have to discover for yourself whether many others are worth growing at home—horseradish, eggplant, potatoes, turnips, spinach, squash, Swiss chard, celery, cauliflower, cabbage and kale and kohlrabi, broccoli and Brussels sprouts. Make a choice if you will—and may you have good luck in finding that extra acre or two of land that you may require!

ASPARAGUS

(*Asparagus officinalis atilis*)

Asparagus in a small garden is a space luxury. But no vegetable gives more taste pleasure when picked fresh. To grow it properly, you should find room in some area where the tall feathery branches will not shade smaller plants during the summer, and where the roots will not be disturbed during the years. New varieties may be chosen that are reliably disease-resistant, sturdy, and productive.

PLANTING: Sixteen one-year roots may be planted about eighteen inches apart in a space two feet by about ten feet. Even four roots will eventually provide several asparagus treats during a season, but it will not be enough!

Spade the bed deeply and supply it with rich compost and manure, if possible, before planting; then scatter lime or wood ashes over it. Set the year-old roots eight inches deep, spread them out carefully, and cover them with soil; then apply a deep mulch of hay, grass clippings, or other light mulch to keep down weed growth. An asparagus bed that is yearly kept richly fertilized, limed, and mulched will be otherwise virtually carefree. However, the shoots cannot compete with growths of other plants, weeds, or grass, so you must either mulch the bed or keep it free of weeds.

Asparagus can be grown from seed instead of roots (the latter will be supplied by many seedsmen and nurseries), but this will delay your first harvest by at least another year.

HARVESTING: The tender young tips of asparagus should not be harvested for two years after plants are put into the ground, which seems a long time to wait. But once ready to be harvested, the bed will then go on producing for many years.

Asparagus is a spring vegetable with a season of approximately six weeks. Stop all cutting of shoots when the stalks begin to seem spindly. Then let the green feathered tops develop and grow all summer in order to store up strength for the following year's harvest. Snap off the shoots when they are about six inches high, or, preferably, cut them with a sharp knife just below the surface of the soil, being careful not to injure underground shoots yet to show.

USES: Asparagus is always best within twenty minutes from garden to table. To cook, snap off the tough ends where they break easily. Wash the spears thoroughly in cold water, removing scales if they contain sand. If necessary, remove sand or dirt with a vegetable brush. Tie spears together with string or hold them together with a band of aluminum foil. Stand spears in a deep narrow pan, in the bottom of a double boiler with top inverted over spears, or a coffeepot, and cook in one inch of boiling water to which ½ teaspoon of salt per cup of water has been added. Cook uncovered for 5 minutes. Cover and cook 7 to 10 minutes longer or until stalk ends are tender but crisp. Drain.

Serve hot with plenty of melted butter, lemon butter, herb butter, or Hollandaise Sauce, for the most delectable early treat of the garden. Cold cooked asparagus makes a delicious salad with oil and vinegar dressing or Sauce Vinaigrette. Cream of asparagus soup and asparagus omelet are gourmet fare, particularly if you add a top garnish of a teaspoonful of fresh chopped herbs. Try asparagus tips on toast topped with cheese sauce and chopped herbs.

This delicious vegetable is well filled with vitamins A and C, and its protein and carbohydrate content is low. It may be canned or frozen, but its fresh quality and flavor are impaired in processing.

GARDEN BEANS

(Chiefly *Phaseolus*)

So many beans are known that they are frequently divided into categories: in the garden, pole beans and bush or dwarf beans; in the kitchen, shell beans or edible-podded beans. They may be classified as green beans or yellow beans, snap beans or wax beans. The Scarlet Runner bean (unfortunately, seldom planted these days) has several different qualities all by itself. It is an ornamental flowering vine, and the beans may be eaten either in the tender pod or shelled.

It used to be necessary to "string" beans by removing ends and pulling off strings that ran along the sides of the pods. These strings have been eliminated in most green and wax beans these days, so refined are the new varieties.

Of all the beans you can grow, the limas (either the baby limas or the large ones), a shell type, are perhaps the most delectable when picked fresh from the kitchen garden. They are called butter beans in the South, and it is a good description of their taste. These beans require at least four months of good warm growing weather for maturity, and so they cannot always be depended upon in the North. Home-grown limas, picked and cooked when absolutely fresh, have superb flavor. Northern gardeners eagerly await the perfection of a fine short-season variety.

PLANTING: In general, you will need a rich deep loam for beans; and you will have to water them during dry spells. Pole beans are usually planted once; when you plant them properly and pick them clean of all ready-to-eat beans each day or two, they will bear for a long time. You should set the poles or trellises on which they must climb before planting the seed. Put the seeds about one inch deep in hills of three or four to a hill, or in a row with seeds about six inches apart. Do not use any but perfect seeds. If you plant more than one row, it is best to space the rows about thirty inches to three feet apart.

Dwarf or bush beans may be planted in succession every two or three weeks from the last frost date in the spring up to August first in the North, later for the South. Beans are not hardy, and the crop is finished with the first fall frost, although you can cover a few of the bush type for protection until that next freeze comes.

HARVESTING: Beans are subject to various diseases, which are easily spread, so never touch the plants when they are wet with rain or dew. The best time to pick beans is when the sun has been shining on them and the foliage is dry. If you must water them, remove the sprinkler nozzle of the hose and let the water run down between the rows.

For best flavor, pick green and wax beans when the pods are tender; some epicures like them quite young. Pick shell beans before they dry and harden but when they have reached full size.

USES: Depending upon the kind of beans, you may choose among many ways of serving them. Basil, dill, marjoram, nutmeg, savory (the "bean herb"), and thyme are good additions to cooked green or wax beans. In casseroles, beans combine well with cheese, mushrooms, onions, almonds, flaked fish, or chopped chicken, turkey, or ham. Lima beans display their own special flavor best when cooked and served with butter, salt, and pepper. They also combine well with parsley, savory, or sage; with cream, lemon butter, or a mild garlic sauce; and baked lima beans with herbs in a casserole are fare for your most elegant buffet supper.

To prepare green or wax beans, wash them in cold water and remove the ends. In crisp young beans, the ends snap off, but you may prefer to cut them with a sharp knife. You may leave the beans whole, or cut them French style into lengthwise strips, or crosswise on a slant into one-inch pieces.

Place beans in one inch salted water (½ teaspoon salt to one cup water. Heat to boiling. *Green:* Cook uncovered 5 minutes. Cover, cook 10-15 minutes whole or cut; 5-10 minutes French style. Drain. *Wax:* Cook covered 15-20 minutes whole or cut; 10-15 minutes French style. Drain.

Shell lima beans just before cooking: remove the thin outer edge of pod with a sharp knife or scissors, and slip the beans out. Place in one inch boiling salted water; cook uncovered for 5 minutes; then cover and cook 15 to 20 minutes longer or until tender. Drain.

SWEET CORN
(*Zea mays rugosa*)

This most American of vegetables is also one of our basic foods. Unfortunately, you must have room to grow enough to supply your family for the summer, although midget types are excellently flavored and good producers. Corn is a stately ornamental plant when well grown. At the back of the kitchen garden try to squeeze in a double row somehow. Corn is better pollinated when grown in two or more rows rather than a single row. If you are one of the lucky people who has eaten sweet corn within twenty minutes of picking in its prime, you know how unbelievably sweet, juicy, buttery, and *tender* corn can be.

PLANTING: If you have plenty of room for planting corn, you can make succession plantings to keep the family supplied until frost. Corn is a heavy feeder. The Indians used to "plant" three herrings or alewives in the ground before planting corn in hills. You can use barnyard, dried cow, or poultry manure at the bottom of your hills or rows and have more and better ears because of it. If you use commercial fertilizer, however, dig it into the soil beside each row.

Plant the seeds about an inch deep, beginning at last frost date (corn is very tender to frost), rather thickly, then thin the plants to twelve to fifteen inches apart, with rows three feet apart. To have early corn, plant the seed in peat pots and transplant the seedlings in their pots after frost date, or when the ground is good and warm.

Although corn loves hot dry days and nights for growing, it also needs water, and in dry times you should give it a good soaking. If you use newer varieties of hybrid seed, you should have disease-free crops. But be sure to keep the ground clean, well cultivated, and free of weeds.

The Indians cultivated corn in fields, one of the few vegetables they bothered to plant in an orderly manner. They also planted pumpkins in the cornfields; later other vine crops such as cucumbers, squash, and watermelon were added. The cartoonists still remind us of the boys who crept in the moonlight among the rows of sweet corn to find the ripest and sweetest watermelons in a farmer's patch.

HARVESTING: Corn is a well-rounded nutritious food. It is at its flavorful best when the juice spurts out of a kernel in response to your testing fingernail. At that point, the silks will be brown but not too dry, the ears well filled out, and the kernels plump and juicy but not too large.

USES: It is great to have enough corn to freeze for the winter. When corn is field-grown and plentiful, one can be assured of it. Frozen, either on the cob, or cut off the cob, corn does lose its fresh sweet flavor, but it is a good nutritious vegetable to serve the family in winter. Yellow corn is rich in vitamin A, and all sweet corn has in addition B_1, B_2, and C, as well as protein, sugar, and starch.

When it is fresh-picked, rush the corn to the kitchen, strip it of husks and silks and put in cold, unsalted water to cover. Heat to boiling. Boil uncovered 2 minutes. Remove from heat. Let corn stand (in pot) for ten minutes. Serve with plenty of butter, salt, and pepper, or with herb butter. Corn that is cut off the cob is delicious creamed; in corn chowder; in relishes or casseroles combined with other vegetables; scalloped; in corn fritters and corn puddings. The Indians made succotash, combining corn and shelled beans, and we do well to cherish their way of serving both of these native American vegetables.

GARDEN PEAS

(*Pisum sativum*)

Garden peas are the nobility of the vegetable families, of timeless antiquity, a bit pampered in the garden, here today and gone tomorow —but glorious while you have them.

PLANTING: Peas are hardy annuals, a cool-weather crop that should be planted very early and in succession until early June (in the North). Elsewhere you can plant early, middle, and late-season varieties all at one time as soon as you can get into the garden in the spring. In a small garden, you may find succession plantings better for they allow a reuse of space. In the deep South peas may be grown in the winter; but they do not flourish anywhere in the heat of summer.

This precious vegetable loves a deeply worked, loamy soil into which you have incorporated liberal amounts of wood ashes. Peas do quite

well without fertilizer if your planting area has been previously composted for growing other things. You may select from dwarf, medium,
and tall sorts. The dwarfs support themselves and need no propping,
but for the medium and tall types you will have to provide netting,
chicken wire, or brush sturdily placed between double rows to support
the vines. Tall varieties will probably produce more peas than the
dwarfs. All peas like moisture, and you might find it best to plant the
seed one to two inches deep in early spring, but two to three inches
deep later in the spring, so that the roots can reach moisture below
ground easily. The plants grow well spaced four to six inches apart.

HARVESTING: Pea pods should be picked from the vines when
pods are bright green and filled from end to end with tender, sweet,
firm peas. When the pods and vines of garden peas begin to change
color and fade, when the pods toughen and the peas become large and
hard, the peas are no longer sweet and good. Then it is time to pull
out the vines and add them to the compost, where they will contribute
valuable nitrogen to the soil.

You need not add sugar to fresh garden peas when you pick and
cook them just before serving, for they contain their own supply of
sugar. However, each moment is precious, and peas that are not prepared immediately for the table soon lose this sugar. So pick them,
cook them, and serve them immediately if possible. Peas may also be
harvested, shelled, blanched, and quick-frozen for later use.

USES: Peas contain vitamins A, B_1, B_2, niacin, and C, as well as protein and carbohydrates. They are truly one of the garden miracles
of flavor when picked fresh and cooked immediately. Many of the

kitchen garden inhabitants combine well with peas, including basil, chervil, chives, marjoram, mint, rosemary, savory, thyme, and tarragon. Peas blend with such vegetables as carrots and tiny onions. A touch of ginger or curry and even a dash of nutmeg makes a delightful change in serving peas. Cooked peas seasoned with salt and pepper and drenched in cream sauce are a delicious old-fashioned country dish.

Cook the shelled peas in not more than one inch of boiling salted water (½ teaspoon salt to 1 **cup water**). Cook them uncovered for 5 minutes, then cover and cook for **an additional** 3 to 7 minutes or until just tender. Drain before adding seasonings or herbs.

Edible-pod peas (which are sometimes appropriately called "sugar peas") are eaten pod, pea, and all, like green beans. They are delicious and well worth growing. Pick them young when you can just feel the newly-formed peas through the pod. Cut the pods crosswise into pieces, then cook in a very little water. Serve with melted butter and a touch of fresh mint or summer savory. Edible-pod peas should not be neglected in our gardens, for they are rich in food value and flavor.

RHUBARB

(*Rheum rhaponticum*)

The correct answer to that old question—is rhubarb a fruit or a vegetable?—is that it is a hardy perennial vegetable. It is usually, however, treated like fruit. The juicy stalks, cut into half-inch pieces and cooked with sugar, make a savory sauce, or they may be used in a pie or jam. Rhubarb may also be made into a wine or punch. A handsome plant when growing, it has rich green leaves that may be quite poisonous to many people and so should *never* be used for anything except composting material.

PLANTING: You may buy rhubarb clumps from many nurseries and seed-supply houses, but you can often coax them from a generous neighbor, for rhubarb does not suffer if roots are cut from a thick stand; in fact, it is often beneficial, especially for old plants. When you have decided where to plant the rhubarb, enrich the soil with a heavy application of compost or manure (dried cow or sheep manure available at garden-supply centers is suitable). Heap manure over the plants in late fall as well, and rake it into the surrounding soil in spring.

Examine the clumps to be sure that the roots have at least three good "eyes" or producing shoots. Then plant the top of the roots two inches below the surface of the soil, and space the plants about four feet apart. Three or four plants will supply an average family during the season, but even one plant means an occasional delicious pie.

HARVESTING: The rhubarb season ceases after about six weeks of harvest. You should pull the stalks gently from the base of the plant (not cut them), and cut off the knobby ends and leaves and compost them. Cut all seedstalks off at the base as they develop, and compost them, because flowering deprives the plant of its vigor.

USES: Rhubarb is high in vitamin C and contains some sugar. If you combine a little chopped angelica with rhubarb in sauce or pie, it will have a tantalizing flavor and will cut down the amount of sugar needed. The best and sweetest rhubarb is the kind with red stalks, and it is also the prettiest to serve. One of the handsomest treats of spring-time is lattice-topped fresh rhubarb pie made with angelica.

To cook rhubarb, cut enough one-inch pieces to measure four cups. Heat ¾ to 1 cup sugar, ½ cup water to boiling; stir occasionally. Add rhubarb. Simmer about 10 minutes or until tender and slightly transparent. Four drops of almond extract add a special flavor.

Tom Thumb Vegetables

Some garden seed catalogs list midget or miniature vegetables for home gardeners with tiny spaces. Among those that are well worth planting, the following well-distributed and easy-to-grow varieties are recommended.

BEANS: Almost any bush bean is suitable for small gardens, if the planting, too, is small. Six or eight plants will give your family several good meals of beans. Larger gardens will have room for more.

CABBAGE: For those who want to try growing miniature cabbages from seed, two varieties are recommended by seedsmen: Dwarf Morden is very sweet and tender, and the heads are about four inches across. Little Leaguer is softball sized, also about four inches.

CARROTS: Short 'n' Sweet and Tiny Sweet are baby carrots that never really grow up and are interesting to try.

CORN: Old reliable Golden Midget is splendid in every way, growing about thirty inches high, with ears four inches long. Another miniature variety is Midget Hybrid, with slightly larger ears than the Golden Midget. There is also a White Midget, sweet and good. You may freeze all of these varieties, although sweet corn is never as good prepared any way other than absolutely fresh.

CUCUMBERS: Cherokee, three plants to a hill, grows into a handsome little bush about three to four feet in diameter and bears full-sized fruit. This is a hybrid plant and resistant to diseases, but it requires plenty of water and extra-rich ground for best production. Tiny Dill has two-foot vines and small fruits that are good for pickling.

LETTUCE: Tom Thumb is a delight to raise and to eat, rich and crisp and buttery in a small head just right for individual servings. It is quick to grow, and you are advised to make succession plantings. This fine small lettuce is wonderful for the indoor, terrace, or child's garden, as well as the larger kitchen garden.

PEAS: Mighty Midget, Little Marvel, and Sparkle peas bear small pods on dwarf bushes for an early sweet treat from the garden.

SQUASH: Gold Nugget and Kindred (an All-America Selection) are excellent rich-yellow dry fruits borne on "bushes" rather than spreading vines. You may grow them in bushel baskets outdoors or in the ground.

TOMATO: Tiny Tim and Small Fry (an All-America Selection) are the best and smallest of the miniature tomatoes. They bear profusely, and their bright scarlet fruits have an excellent vine-ripe tomato flavor. You can grow them indoors in winter, outdoors in summer.

Midget watermelons, eggplants, and pumpkins are also listed in some catalogs. Constant experiments are being conducted to find good-quality tiny vegetables for small gardens, and each year's seed catalogs will undoubtedly carry new varieties well worth trying in any kitchen garden, large or small.

Chapter 7

The Little Gardens

To have nothing here but Sweet Herbs
And those only choice ones, too.
                    —ERASMUS, 1500

"I GIARDINETTI"

ONE WHO LOVES TO GROW and use herbs took a walk in The City on a summer afternoon. From a cobble-paved narrow street an arched door-way, which somehow said Welcome without spelling the word on any kind of sign, led into a tiny courtyard surrounded on all sides by four- and five-storied apartment buildings of another era. On the ground level the courtyard was an enchanting green garden of aromatic shrubs and herbs. The soft splash of water from a weathered cherub fountain, and an antique iron garden bench, were an invitation to rest for a few precious quiet moments in the center of the great City.

On a fourth-floor balcony high above, facing south, a long window box was braced securely on the wrought-iron railing, and there grew a kitchen garden, spilling its tender sweet herbs luxuriantly over the edges of the balcony. "I know who lives there," the visitor rejoiced— "someone who cooks with herbs and wine and flair." From form, color, and leaves she named the plants—rosemary, sage, marjoram, basil, thyme, tarragon, chives, and parsley. In the shadow of the box, on the floor of the tiny balcony (big enough for supper for two) was a small wooden tub filled with mint. In a hanging basket suspended from a hook in the door frame, Tiny Tim tomatoes flamed in the sunshine. A kitchen garden of *fines herbes* and *bouquets garnis* on a fourth-floor balcony in the center of The City!

Kitchen gardens do not have to be measured in feet or yards or acres. They can be measured in inches just as successfully. Grown in pots or boxes in a sunny place, indoors or outdoors, winter or summer, they are bounded only by the enthusiasm and patience of the gardener and the amount of sunlight (or even suitable artificial light) that can be made available.

The Italians have a charming word for them—*I Giardinetti,* "little gardens." Such little gardens give happy pleasure to their owners, providing flavoring, fragrance, and decoration as satisfying to those with limited space as larger gardens. Whether planted indoors or outdoors, the little gardens make few demands, but of course these few are important. Actually, garden plants take no more care—sometimes much less care—than do ordinary houseplants. But the rewards are beyond measure.

DEMANDS OF THE LITTLE GARDENS

First, little gardens ask plenty of sunlight or adequate artificial light. Second, plants want enough water and humidity, but not wet feet, and some fresh air. Third, they need good rich soil, because plants grown in containers exhaust the nutriments of soil more quickly than plants grown in the ground. And last, they want good garden-keeping, which means keeping the plants tidy by removing faded leaves and insects. For herbs, it means using the foliage for the kitchen, so that the plants stay bushy and trim.

The most difficult indoor requirement to maintain is sufficient light in winter. To equal the long growing days of summer, you should provide twelve to fourteen hours of good light. This is impossible unless you augment the winter sunlight hours with artificial light. Herbs positively thrive indoors on this much light, but they may also do reasonably well with whatever natural sunlight is available in a south window. Remember though that most herbs originated in lands where warmth and light are abundant.

Experts in the art of growing plants have come to the rescue of would-be indoor gardeners. They have devised attractively mounted lights with shelves and trays that can be a decorative feature of any room in the house, whether or not the sun ever reaches it—even a dark hallway. Complete directions for growing plants in this way come with the fixtures, which you may buy through advertisements in garden magazines and from garden catalogs, garden-supply houses, and specialty plant departments of many stores. Once you have experience in growing plants with such lights you will have learned many tricks in adjusting the space between plants and light to secure best growth. The lighted trays are very useful in starting seeds in pots or flats for spring gardening, and kits that have all the necessary equipment may often be bought with the lights.

You can grow plants with some success under 60- to 75-watt bulbs in household fixtures, should this be more practical for some individual plants. With this method, a pot of rosemary will flourish exceedingly if you augment the day's sunlight by the light of a floor lamp in evening, or a pot of marjoram will benefit if you put it under a table lamp. You may have beauty and fragrance in the bathroom from herbs placed on a shelf under a good constant light. And in the bedroom, sweet herbs will be a refreshing addition if you give them sunlight or artificial light with the necessary moisture and growing temperatures.

Many American homes are too hot and too dry for growing herbs successfully indoors, but you can remedy this condition easily. To provide sufficient humidity around the plants, set them in pots or boxes in a tray of pebbles. Keep the water level in the tray just at the top of the stones. This provides moderately cool, fresh, moist air around the plants. If you spray them with an occasional mist of clear water the plants will also benefit. You can buy suitable inexpensive plastic atomizers for this purpose in garden centers. Such a mist spraying once or twice a week also helps the plant resist insect pests that may attack in a too-hot, dry atmosphere. These humidity precautions for the plants will provide a healthier humidity for your family too.

Water the plant whenever the top of the soil is dry to the touch. Believe it or not, plants, like people, resent chemically treated city water, and they prefer their air and their water *au naturel*. If you can obtain rainwater or filtered water, use that, at room temperature. But herbs—again like people—are long-suffering and may do reasonably well on many types of city water, as long as the chlorine content is not too high.

The temperature at which you grow herbs indoors also has much to do with their successful progress. You can achieve a good temperature range if you keep a room at 70° or below during the day, lowering the heat at night to not more than 60°.

The third requirement for growing kitchen garden plants indoors is rich soil. Most supermarkets and variety stores, sometimes even drug and hardware stores, carry potting soil in various-sized packages. To these prepared mixes add some bone meal for nutriment, plus sand mixed with a little lime or wood ashes. Look in pet shops for boxes of fine sharp sand mixed with ground oystershells for use in birdcages. This is excellent to add to prepared potting soil—the sand helps lighten the mixtures and the oystershells provide the necessary lime, adding two desirable ingredients to the soil.

If you have a supply of potting materials available in your outdoor garden, make a mixture of three parts of good rich soil and compost, one part sand, a little bone meal, and wood ashes or lime. You should find this an excellent mix for the indoor garden.

During the late-winter indoor growing season, when the daylight begins to stretch to longer hours, a very light application of balanced commercial fertilizer may be helpful to compensate for the continual harvesting of leaves or tips. Apply it not oftener than once a month. Repot plants grown in containers at least once a year, in the fall (and, even better, in the spring as well).

Herbs indoors like growing room, which means that the pots in which you grow them should be five or six inches across the top. Clay pots are best. They allow the soil within them to breathe, and water slowly evaporates through them so that the plants are not so apt to have wet feet. If you grow the herbs in boxes, the depth of the box should be at least eight or nine inches, and you should give each plant spreading room.

CONTAINERS FOR LITTLE GARDENS

All containers used for growing herbs should have good drainage. Holes in the bottom of window boxes and pots, which are then set on pebbles in trays containing water, provide the best means of drainage. You can paint the trays and boxes to match the trim color of the room. You may also set individual clay pots into more ornamental glazed containers, providing you lift the pots off the bottom of such containers with a layer of small stones, or even bottle caps, to keep the clay pot out of the water.

You can be quite fancy-free when choosing ornamental containers for little gardens. If you would like a convenient selection of herbs for gourmet cooking, you could put your choice of *fines herbes* into a hanging basket, or into a wooden cheesebox such as those in which wheels of cheese are delivered to grocers and delicatessens, or in a strawberry jar. These would be attractive not only indoors, but on a terrace in the summer as well. Various jars, pots, and tubs may be used, whatever is available and suits your taste. You do have to be a little watchful not to achieve a too-cluttered or "cute" look with such containers.

You will probably find that plants grown in containers need a little more grooming than those in the ground—they are the prima ballerinas, as it were, of the garden. Nip off dead leaves and blossoms whenever you find them, and snip the herb tops frequently for kitchen use, to keep plants bushy and full. Their beauty is lost when they become straggly and go to seed.

Container plants that are moved out of doors in the spring will give an otherwise ordinary corner of your garden a special interest and charm. You may place fragrant herbs so that their aroma reaches those passing by, and herbs around the family cookout center where they will be useful as well as beautiful. A special attribute of herbs in containers is the ease with which they can be moved around the garden, where they will be happiest in sunlight or shade, most useful for snipping or for fragrance, or provide the greatest pleasure.

GREEN THUMB TIPS

During November, December, and even into January, it is not likely that any of the herbs will flourish indoors as they would in summer out of doors, for all plants like some rest period. But the successful little gardener will snip judiciously during these months and will attend to the wants of the plants until new green tips are again coaxed into full growth.

To keep the plants from becoming leggy in their reach for sunlight, turn those grown in a window by one-quarter each time you water them. If their boxes are heavy, turning once a week will help. Herbs respond, too, if you wash the plants and the pots now and then in tepid water.

Do not cut off an entire plant at once if you want it to remain alive, especially in the house. Plants grow through their leaves as well as their roots, and to denude a whole plant often kills it. So use snippings in the kitchen, not whole branches.

For best growth in winter, you should not permit herbs to produce flowers, except for the scented geraniums and rosemary. Snip out the flower buds (most can be used in cooking, as well as the leaves), and the plant will devote its energy to producing more and better leaves.

If the plants are in a window during a sudden very cold spell, draw the curtains at night between plants and window, or place a sheet of newspaper against the window to keep cold drafts and frost from injuring tender leaves.

If red spider mites, scale insects, or whiteflies infest the plants when grown indoors (or outdoors for that matter), you can control them with occasional spraying of a mist of cool water and alcohol. To make the spray add one or two tablespoonsful of rubbing alcohol to each pint of water. Use it once a week (but not when plants are in full sun) until the infestation disappears. Commercial sprays must be used with extreme care, if at all, indoors and on any plants used as food.

On warm, sunny days, you may set the plants outside for a welcome sunbath and some fresh air; or on warm rainy days, you can give them a good outdoor soaking of beneficial rain—which contains valuable nitrogen for green growing things.

If the leaves of herbs become faded and plants are drooping, check your watering habits and try changing plant locations to give them different light and temperature and more room.

BRINGING IN PLANTS FROM OUTDOORS

You may be fortunate enough to have an outdoor garden from which to garner your supply of herbs for indoor growing in winter. For transferring such plants, here are a few helpful tricks.

Small young plants take more kindly to being potted for indoor growing than large plants. You will find it best to plant seeds or make cuttings in late August or September of those herbs that you may want for winter gardens. When the seedlings reach about three inches, take them from the seeding place and put them into their indoor containers. Bring them indoors gradually, by leaving them in the warm autumn sunshine and rain during the day but carrying them indoors on cool nights.

Most of the perennial herbs may be potted as cuttings or small plants in the fall and brought indoors gradually to the light and warmth of the window garden. Change this procedure slightly for chives, mint, and tarragon, as suggested below and on pages 44, 55, and 70.

SUITABLE PLANTS FOR LITTLE GARDENS

Many kitchen garden plants flourish indoors in plant boxes or pots in limited spaces, but some do have special characteristics for indoor growing. You need not limit your choice of plants to those which follow, however; experimenting is part of the fun.

Miniature fruit trees make charming potted plants for little gardens, indoors or outdoors. They furnish welcome blossoms and fruit the year around. Among these are the miniature oranges, the fruits of which may grow to about one inch in diameter. This orange is bitter, but it makes a fine garnish (roast duck a l'orange, or old-fashioned cocktails, for example), can be candied, and makes an excellent marmalade. Two small fruit trees in handsome paired pots may be used as decorative accents in your house or garden. They need no special care except sunlight, enough moisture, and good soil. If scale attacks their leaves, that is, if you find tiny hard-shelled spots on the backs of the leaves (the scale insect lives under these while sucking the juice from the leaves), scrape them off with a fingernail, and spray the plant with an alcohol-water mist as suggested on page 131.

Miniature lemon, lime, pomegranate, and kumquat trees, as well as the dwarf fig, are excellent little garden plants. You may set any of these outside in the warm seasons; and in areas of the South you may leave them out of doors the year around.

Basil seeds may be planted at any time for use in the indoor little garden, sown directly into a pot. Sow several seeds and thin them to one sturdy plant. Basil likes a warm place and does beautifully in a sunny kitchen window. For low bushy growth, use the tips of branches quite generously. Do not permit the plant to flower because it will complete its growth cycle and then die. To prevent flowering, keep pinching out the blossom buds. Basil stems are easily rooted in water or sand for indoor planting.

Salad burnet makes a pretty houseplant with its dainty leaves and graceful trailing stems. This herb is excellent in hanging baskets or on shelves where the light is good. Start it, if possible, from seeds planted in August or September. You may set it into the garden in spring.

Chervil germinates rapidly from seeds sown in the fall and the plant completes its growth cycle quickly. So make several seedings in pots or boxes during the winter for continued use in salads or for garnish.

Chives flourish indoors. If you bring a mature plant from the garden to the indoor kitchen garden for winter use, dig and pot the plant in the fall, and sink the pot into the ground for a month or two of winter dormancy. Then cut it back, give it a little drink of manure tea or liquid balanced fertilizer, and bring it into indoor warmth and sunlight for a winter of snippings. If it is not possible to provide this dormant period for a plant dug from a garden, sow chive seeds in a five-inch pot for quick and easy indoor windowsill use. Put the resulting plant out

of doors if desired when spring comes—it will grow and spread in the outdoor garden. Plants bought in markets usually need to be repotted in larger containers, allowing plenty of rich soil and room.

Garden cress, sometimes called upland cress, may be sown into a flat or a box. Its spicy sharp flavor will provide welcome fresh greens that you may add to salads or use as a garnish. Make succession sowings all winter, because the whole plants are cut off at the roots for kitchen use. Cress likes sunshine and damp soil, and wintertime would be a good time to test the wet-blotter method for planting and raising it (see page 82).

Dill seed may be sown directly into a pot or box. You may allow several plants to develop in a single five- or six-inch pot. Growing quickly indoors, it remains small and neat, rather than stretching into the tall spindly plant of the outdoor garden. Dill leaves are excellent in salads, sauces, and sandwiches, and for canapés and hors d'oeuvres.

Garlic cloves may be planted in a pot so that you may snip the tips for use like chives. Put the cloves into a rich soil and a sunny warm place.

Lemon balm (a cousin of the kitchen garden mints, with the lovely botanical name of *Melissa officinalis*), not one of the most important kitchen garden herbs, tends to make a trailing growth when planted indoors. Thus it makes a desirable plant for pots, hanging baskets, or boxes where it can trail over the edge. In a sunny window or under a light in the bathroom, it freshens the room and adds sweetness to the air. You may even throw its leafy tips into your bath water to provide a delightful fragrance. If you grow it in other rooms, you may find its leaves are delicious for tea and in cocktails that are enhanced by a pleasant lemony-mint taste. Dig a small plant from the garden in fall and cut it back two-thirds for bringing indoors; or sow seed directly into a pot.

Marjoram becomes a trailing plant indoors, quite different from its perky upright outdoor growth. Dig it before frost and cut it back to two-thirds; or plant seeds directly into a pot in the early fall. You may use the tips quite generously in the kitchen. Provide warmth and plenty of sunlight, and see that it does not have wet feet.

Mint likes a cool room and does well in only partial sunlight. Do put it in a pot or tub by itself because it would soon take over a window box with its spreading roots. If possible, purchase, or dig from the garden, a small young plant that has been newly grown from seed, from layerings, or root cuttings. If you dig a mature plant from the garden to bring indoors, pot it, as on page 55. When you bring it indoors, it will start growing for garnish and flavoring all winter. As explained in the case of chives, some mature herbs (tarragon is another) require this treatment for really successful indoor performance.

Parsley will not do well unless it is in a deep container, because it has a long taproot that needs length of pot room. Put it in a *cool* sunny place and do not add fertilizer during the winter, once it is potted. If you use the outside leaves generously, the new growth will remain healthy and vigorous. When parsley does not seem to thrive, a change of location is often the answer to its problems. Seed planted in a deep pot or box takes several weeks to germinate, but succession sowings may provide a larger supply of leaves if you find that one plant is not enough.

Rose geranium (or any scented geranium) plants or rooted cuttings will thrive all winter, and may bloom, if kept in a sunny window. You may use the leaves constantly for refreshing tea and for garnishing cakes and fruit dishes. Although sun is necessary, geraniums like a rather cool situation.

Rosemary must be brought indoors for winter in the North. It makes a delightful houseplant, a conversation piece, and a source of constant pleasure to the cook. Cut it back lightly before bringing it into the house. The size of a rosemary plant will often depend on the size of its container, and in a large pot you may grow a sizable shrub. If you want smaller plants, let the plants become pot-bound to keep down their growth. Rosemary must have adequate watering, although it will not live in constantly soggy soil. If you let the roots dry out completely even once, the plant will curl up the edges of its leaves, turn yellow, and die. When the top of the soil is dry to the touch, water well, and leave it until it again feels dry. Rosemary loves a warm, sunny place, and in a picture window becomes a plant of special beauty and enjoyment. Because dried or frozen rosemary leaves do not retain a desirable flavor and fragrance, you should keep a plant indoors for winter use.

Sage flourishes best when you dig a small plant from the garden, or start it from seed in the fall. It is an attractive, aromatic indoor plant, and its fresh leaves may be used judiciously for seasoning. But do not harvest a large quantity of sage from an indoor plant at any one time. You may also get sage leaves from plants in the outdoor garden in the winter, even if they are covered with snow. For quantity use in dressings and stuffings, however, harvest and dry garden sage during the outdoor growing season. It is an old remedy for colds when used in a tea.

Winter savory is useful indoors if you dig a plant from the garden or sow seeds in the fall for winter plants. You may pick some winter savory, like sage, from the garden during most winter months. Put it in a cool sunny location indoors, and use its leaves in stews, meat dishes, soups, and gravies.

Sweet bay trees are fine decorative accents in little gardens, indoors, out-of-doors. You will have to bring them in before frost because they do not survive the cold. Snip their leaves judiciously all winter for use in cooking. Plants must be purchased or started from cuttings, and it usually takes a long time to root such cuttings, so the plants are apt to be more expensive than most herbs, but they are well worth the price.

Tarragon is a must for the indoor little garden, as it is for the outdoor kitchen garden. You may purchase a young plant in the fall, or

root a stem cutting from a mature plant or put layered rootings from garden-grown plants into pots to bring indoors. Remember that true tarragon does not grow from seed, only from stem or root cuttings. These newly rooted cuttings do not require the period of dormancy that mature tarragon plants must have if they are to do well for winter indoor growing, as explained above for chives and mint. A tarragon plant will do well in a pot or basket by itself, or in a box of *fines herbes* for one season. Put it in a warm sunny place.

Thyme thrives indoors if it is not kept too wet—a common fault of indoor herb gardens. You may start it easily from seed, or lift a young small plant or rooted layering from the garden for indoor use. It likes a warm sunny location, and although it tends to trail when brought indoors, it flourishes when you snip the stem tips frequently for culinary uses.

Tiny Tim tomato plants grown in hanging baskets or in pots are a most satisfactory addition to your little garden. Indoors, when blossoms start developing, shake the branches gently once a day to provide fertilization of the blossoms. With care, you will get tiny succulent red tomatoes, so desirable for salads, garnishes, and for occasional fresh tomato bites. Tomato plants require plenty of bright sunshine, warmth, and water for flourishing growth and production. They are sometimes afflicted with aphids or red spider mites indoors; but you can control them rather easily (see page 131).

Tiny onions grow in a small flat with rich soil; mustard seed or cress or rocket may be scattered in a flat or box for a taste of crisp tangy salad green. Root climbing nasturtiums in water and grow them in a warm sunny window all winter; add a piece of charcoal to keep the water fresh and add more water as needed to the container. What excitement when you can serve Tom Thumb lettuce plants, grown indoors, whole on a salad plate. Such little garden extravagances as these boost any city dweller's self-esteem and morale, to say nothing of the boost to your reputation as a cook and gardener.

Early fall is really the time to plan and plant winter little gardens. Sow the parsley seed, pot the chives, put the mint to bed for a short time. Bring in the bay and the orange tree or the rosemary; cut back the marjoram and thyme and put them into handsome pots. Move the curtains back in the south windows (or take them down!), let all the sunshine pour in, and start enjoying the winter little garden.

Chapter 8

The Merry-Go-Round Garden

No one in the family should be deprived of his own garden corner, and the Merry-Go-Round Garden is dedicated to the children. It is made with a wagon wheel, which will probably necessitate a family Sunday in the country. Take a picnic lunch, and scout around farmyards with ancient and weatherbeaten barns, search through antique shops, or look for barn sales where you can inquire about wagon or buggy wheels for this very special garden.

A wheel suitable for the Merry-Go-Round could have eight or sixteen spokes; if you have sixteen, saw half of them out to make the eight sections needed. Of course, a wheel with a different number of spokes would be just as acceptable, but you would have to make a few changes in the planting plan suggested to accommodate the number of spaces in your wheel.

Let the young master or mistress of the garden decide which wheel is preferred; if it is to be painted blue or red or yellow; if it is to be a tiny one or an extra-big one. Tie the wheel on top of the car or slide it in the back of the station wagon, or lash it firmly to the side of the family bus; and bring it home in triumph.

When garden spading day comes, lay the wheel on the ground in its designated place, and with a sharp spade cut into the turf all around the outside edge. Remove the wheel for the time being, and cut out all the turf within the circle's rim; turn the turf upside down in the compost pile, or repair eroded lawn spots with it. Then pile fertile compost or peat moss plus dried cow manure, lime, or wood ashes (and if the soil is heavy, a bucket of sand) in the center of the circle. Spade it in deeply. With the sharp spade again, go around the rim of the

Find a place in your garden that the
children can call their own.

The young gardener enjoys seeing results quickly.

garden the depth of the spade, cutting a place to insert a length of the metal edging that may be found in hardware stores and garden-supply shops. This edging will keep grass from encroaching into the circle. Bury it just to the top of the soil.

The young gardener will then want to take a small light rake and rake the soil of this garden finely and evenly. When the moment comes to lay the wheel back onto the plot, everyone pitches in for the "foundation laying," with the young garden planner directing operations. Let him firm the wheel by walking on the spokes (a neat balancing act), and then water down the soil with the spray nozzle of the hose. It is good at this point to let the soil settle for a few days—perhaps in the meantime a good rain or another sprinkling will help to settle it even more.

Have eight inviting packets of seed ready, and help the gardener make his labels. Fine Merry-Go-Round labels can be made by rinsing out and opening up a two-quart waxed milk carton. With animal cooky

Merry~Go~Round Garden

(MADE WITH A WAGON WHEEL)

Wheel diagram (clockwise from top):

"BROWNIE SCOUT"

MARIGOLDS

"LEMON DROP" or "BROWNIE"

SCOUT

MARIGOLDS

"LEMON DROP" or "BROWNIE"

Sections:
- Cherry Belle Radishes
- Dill *
- Beets
- Chives
- "Tiny Sweet" Carrots
- "Tom Thumb" Lettuce
- Onion Sets or Garlic Buds
- Chervil *

Center: Tiny Tim Tomatoes

Let some go to seed to self-sow all summer.

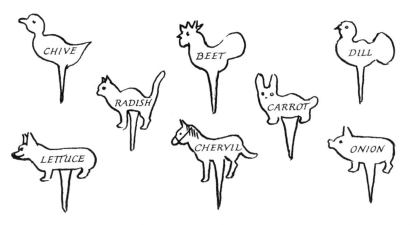

CHIVE · BEET · DILL · RADISH · CARROT · LETTUCE · CHERVIL · ONION

8 Labels in Shapes of Cooky Cutter Animals

cutters shaped like a horse, bird, lamb, duck, giraffe, boy, lion, elephant, or anything handy, draw eight shapes, and cut them from the carton. On the unprinted side of the cardboard, using a waterproof felt-tip pen, write the names of the seeds to be planted. Staple these shapes to ice-cream sticks, tongue depressors, or thin wooden garden labels. The labels are then ready to stick firmly into the ground at the rim of the wheel, one for each section. Seed-packet pictures could be stapled on the sticks in place of the animal cutouts, if that would make it easier for the child to identify the planting.

For impatient young gardeners, seeds should be planted that will show results quickly. Follow directions on the seed packets for planting and thinning. Cherry Belle radish; dill; chervil, which tastes like licorice and is delicious to snip and snack; chives; Tiny Sweet carrots, a midget variety; Tom Thumb lettuce; onion sets or garlic sections; and beets are suggested. Around the rim of the wheel, Lemondrop or Brownie Scout marigolds will make the garden gay and help to keep insects away. On the hub of the wheel, a single plant of Tiny Tim tomatoes in a pot will soon be showing blossoms and then the miniature fruit that is so great a reward for the waiting!

It is a pleasure to watch children carefully put the seed into the soil and patiently cover it up. They watch with pride and growing excitement as the seed sprouts and burgeons. They enjoy the fragrance, the taste, and the textures of plants in their own tiny kitchen gardens. Such a garden will encourage a youngster to take pride in his own horticultural achievements, which of course will be much greater than those of anyone else in the family. And think of the material for "Show and Tell" at school!

If a wheel is not available, you can simulate the wheel pattern with bricks, stones, or shells.

A Fireman's Garden can be made similarly by using an old wooden ladder (it will not matter what shape it is in for no one will be climbing it) for the planting bed.

These two minigardens may also be adapted by grown-ups to provide small spaces for growing a few special herbs.

Chapter 9

Something New for Each Day

What neat repast shall feast us, light and choice?
—John Milton (1608–1674)

A STROLL THROUGH the kitchen garden will give abundant pleasure and pride in what you have grown. And while you are strolling (with a basket to gather goodies), choose an assortment of herbs and vegetables to grace the table as a centerpiece for a welcome change. Flower arrangements made from the kitchen garden are unusual and charming additions to a festive dinner. They often have the added virtue of being edible. One of your favorites could be a low yellow mixing bowl filled with a green cushion of parsley, into which you have carefully poked any one of the flowers that are available in the garden—chives, marigolds, or calendulas, giant pansies, nasturtiums. Or what could be saucier than an arrangement made with green herbs and colorful vegetables? A "tussie-mussie" (see Glossary, page 163) of herbs, with a blossom in the center, is a challenge to those gathered at table—how many can be identified? Boutonnieres of herbs on the folded napkin beside each plate are a thoughtful and fragrant touch.

If it is true that variety is the spice of life, it is inversely and even more delightfully evident that spice can make the variety of life. The spice of herbs and fresh vegetables from your own kitchen garden provide excitement and change to the day-by-day preparation of meals for the family and for guests that takes cooking out of the same old routine.

Kitchen garden vegetables are crisp, sweet, colorful, and filled with good health and well-being. The herbs enhance and enrich the natural flavor of foods in addition to adding a sparkle of their own. Herbs and vegetables, herbs and meats or fish, herbs and salads, even herbs and desserts—they all go together like pine trees and the sky, mountain brooks and trout.

It is a temptation to say that there is a definite formula for using fresh as against the dried herbs, as so many books direct and as recipes often specify. It is better to treat such formulas as suggestions, rather than directions. For *it all depends.* Whether dried herbs are stronger than fresh depends on many things, and you will learn to judge for yourself.

It depends, for one thing, on when you pick your fresh herbs. If you gather them in the heat of the day in bright sunlight, the leaves will not have the full flavor of those picked as their flower buds are opening when the air is cool in the morning or early evening. If dried herbs have been processed with care, their flavor *will* be much more intense than the more delicate flavor of the fresh, and so you should use them differently from the fresh. If you have carefully processed your own herbs within the year and have kept them stored in a cool dry dark place in airtight jars, their flavor will be much greater than herbs that may have been too-long exposed to light and heat. Herbs stored carefully in the whole leaf also retain the fragrant oils much more successfully than herbs ground to a fine powder when harvested.

So, *it depends.* In hot foods it is safe and wise to try a pinch first, then to taste, and to add more if necessary. Soon your own pattern of taste will develop. In cold foods, such as salad dressings, marinades, butters, cheese spreads, and aspics or gelatins, herbs added ahead of time will give the food a chance to acquire a more distinct flavor.

One of the statements often seen in print on the use of herbs is: Never use herbs in more than one dish at a meal. Why not? It would be difficult to draw any lines, and it is true that too much herbism in one meal may very well spoil the whole. But if the herbs are properly used, there is no reason why you should not use an herb or two in the casserole as well as in the salad; or in the soup as well as in the meat; in the hors d'oeuvres as well as the dessert. A good cook would not put

the same herb in everything, nor would he (or she) put herbs in every dish in one meal. But to make too many ironclad rules about herbs is to spoil the fun of learning about them and using them. Try and taste. Enjoy and repeat. Many of the great dishes the world has known were innovations made by breaking some kind of culinary rule. There is something new for each day in the use of herbs.

The first American cookbook, published in 1796 by Miss Amelia Simmons, devoted forty-seven pages to recipes using American vegetables and meats, and many of the recipes contained at least one herb—thyme, sweet marjoram, summer savory, sage, parsley, and pennyroyal being her favorites, "uſeful in Cookery." She called for "water-creſſes" to garnish the roast mutton; "greenparſley" with the roast veal and lamb; and her turkey dressing contained "ſweet marjoram, ſummer ſavory, parſley and ſage and ſome add a gill of wine." Miss Simmons' little book contained a word brand new to housewives of that time—"cookey"—which was a rolled and baked sweet dough theretofore called cake. Her recipe for this first American "cookey" contained the seed of an herb that grew in most colonial kitchen gardens, coriander. "Add two large ſpoons of finely powdered coriander ſeed," she advised in old-fashioned print (the old-style s [ſ] was used at the beginning or within a word). "Bake fifteen or twenty minutes in a ſlack oven—good for three weeks."

So do cookbooks today abound with splendid uses for kitchen garden herbs in every part of a meal from hors d'oeuvres to dessert. For good measure in these pages, a few suggestions are added here to encourage and interest readers to experiment with herbs in favorite ways of their own.

A Collation of Herbal Culinary Terms

BOUQUET GARNI

Bouquet garni and *fines herbes* are French expressions found more and more often in American directions for cooking. A *bouquet garni* is a blend of sprigs of fresh or dried herbs tied together and used in marinades or cooked with the foods, then removed before serving soups, stews, gravies, boiled or poached meats and fish. If sprigs are not available, tie the dried leaves into little cheesecloth bags, which, like the *bouquets*, should be removed before serving the food. A sweet bay leaf or piece of one is nearly always included in a *bouquet garni* (unless a recipe should specify otherwise), and usually sprigs of parsley, thyme, basil, savory, marjoram, or chervil in various combinations.

Many recipes suggest putting the *bouquet* into the pot no matter how long the cooking period is to be. However, the flavor is less apt to boil away in the steam if the *bouquet* is added within the last 15 to 25 minutes of cooking when you are poaching or making stews and soups.

COURT BOUILLON

Many recipes for fish and shellfish direct that the fish be poached or boiled in a "court bouillon." This literally means "short clear soup," and one might further define it as a clear flavored soup in which fish or other seafoods are briefly cooked until done. The soup is best made of fish trimmings, including bones and heads (not the innards), flavored with spices and herbs. Strain it before placing the fish in it. Whole fish, or large pieces of fish, or shellfish such as shrimps or lobster may be poached in it.

Kitchen garden herbs and vegetables that add flavor to a court bouillon are onion, thinly sliced or diced carrot, crushed clove of garlic, "a pinch of thyme," and a *bouquet garni* containing lovage, bay leaf, parsley, and a little dill or fennel seed.

After the fish has been cooked, you may use the strained bouillon that remains in the preparation of sauces, or you may freeze it for use on another day.

FINES HERBES

Generally speaking, *fines herbes* (meaning, of course, "fine herbs") are any delicate blend of several minced fresh herbs, which for best flavor are added to the dishes in the last few minutes of cooking, or as a top garnish. These herbs traditionally are parsley, tarragon, chives, and chervil in various combinations and quantities of two, three, or four herbs. They are used especially in sauces, soups, and gravies, in egg and cheese dishes, and in marinades. Experimenting with *fines herbes* using your own combinations and quantities in recipes will often provide delightful changes. You might add any of the sweet herbs to the list, such as basil, marjoram, thyme, and rosemary. Some are so well defined in flavor that you would be wise to use them in less than equal quantities with more delicate herbs. In a bowl of salad, instead of the traditional group, you might try 2 teaspoons of dill leaves, one teaspoon each of parsley and chives. In tomato dishes, perhaps two parts basil to one part each of marjoram and thyme would be interesting; in an omelet, try two pinches of parsley to one each of tarragon and marjoram.

HERB BUTTERS

Many cookbooks contain recipes for making herb butter, and they are as varied as the kinds of herbs that grow, as are their uses. An herb butter is a combination of butter and chopped fresh green herbs. Dried herbs can also be used, about ½ teaspoonful of the dried being the usually recommended equivalent for 1 tablespoonful of the fresh green herbs, or to taste (see page 143). The butters should mellow several hours or overnight in the refrigerator to bring out the flavor of the herbs.

RECIPE FOR HERB BUTTER

Bring one stick (¼ pound) of butter to room temperature; then with a wooden spoon work in 2 to 3 teaspoonsful (or to your taste) of any one fresh green herb (or about ½ teaspoonful of dried herb, see above) and a dash of lemon juice. If desired, with some herbs, a crushed half of a garlic clove can be added. When thoroughly mixed, the herb butter is molded into containers. Try using old brown or yellow custard cups, which hold just the right amount and are pretty enough to put on the table if you like. Cover with plastic film and refrigerate for several hours or overnight to mellow before using.

These butters impart delightful flavor. A list of all the uses would be pages long, so varied are they. Try these for a start:

BASIL BUTTER: Use in any hot tomato dish, on eggs, on roast Cornish hen or any kind of game, on pea or bean soup.

CHIVE BUTTER: Use on almost anything hot, including all the dishes suggested here.

DILL BUTTER: Use on boiled, mashed, or baked potatoes; broiled salmon steaks; scrambled eggs; seafood casseroles.

Fines Herbes Butter: Use on any hot vegetables. On fresh sweet corn it is one of the best reasons for having a kitchen garden!

PARSLEY BUTTER: Use on vegetables, fish, potatoes, and for making Hollandaise and Béarnaise sauces.

SAVORY BUTTER: Use on green or wax beans, beets, and boiled summer squash or zucchini; to top a poached egg, to sauté frankfurters, chops, or steaks.

TARRAGON BUTTER: Use on broiled lobster, sautéed mushrooms, Eggs Benedict, fried trout.

THYME BUTTER: Use in stuffings, gravy, on pork chops; on hot vegetables; on any hot soup or stew.

And so could the list go on and on—as long as your imagination holds out.

HERBED FLOUR

A glass pint jar in the cupboard will hold herbed flour for use in dusting chicken or chops for frying, or making gravies or sauces. The recipe for the herbed flour is 2 cups of flour, 1 to 2 teaspoons of minced dried herbs, ½ teaspoon salt, and some freshly ground pepper. This flavorful flour can also be used for making biscuits, dumplings, or pizza crust.

HERB JELLIES

Herb jellies may be made with apples as a base, or they may be made with prepared pectin (bottled or powder form). Some of the jellies are especially good served with poultry and meats, such as mint, basil, thyme, marjoram, or tarragon jellies. Others, such as rose geranium or

rose petal jelly, are delightful additions to—of all things—a peanut butter sandwich in your youngster's favorite lunch. Or try them on hot biscuits, toast, pancakes, or crêpes.

Jellies made of lemon verbena, scented geranium leaves, or rose petals, lemon balm, lavender, or rosemary leaves are unusual and delicate. In pretty jars, they make the nicest sort of hostess gifts, or gifts for special occasions, or gifts for someone who needs a lift of spirits as well as taste.

You can produce a delicate herb flavor in any fruit jelly by putting a leaf or small sprig of an herb into the jar after pouring in the jelly.

A leaf or two of mint, for instance, is delicious to top glasses of currant or grape jelly. An easy way in which to make herb jellies is to follow the instructions for mint jelly (using the herb of your choice) that come with all prepared pectins. Add a few drops of vegetable coloring if you like.

The following recipe for herb jelly produces a jelly mingling the flavors of fruit and herbs in an appealing way.

RECIPE FOR HERB JELLY

2 tablespoons herb or spice:

    for orange juice—fresh marjoram leaves

    for tangerine juice—whole cloves

    for grape juice—fresh tarragon leaves

2 cups boiling water

1 can (6 ounces) frozen orange, tangerine, or grape juice concentrate, thawed

1 package (1¾ ounces) powdered fruit pectin

3¾ cups sugar

Wash, rinse, and sterilize jelly glasses. Keep glasses in the hot water until ready for use. About 5 minutes before the end of the jelly's cooking period, remove glasses from water and invert on folded towel to drain.

Wrap herbs securely in cheesecloth and place in saucepan with boiling water. Cover; let stand 10 minutes. To extract flavor, squeeze cheesecloth into water. Measure herb water and add enough water to measure 2 cups.

Stir juice, fruit pectin, and herb water in saucepan until pectin is dissolved. Stirring constantly, cook over high heat until mixture comes to rolling boil, about 2 minutes. Add sugar; heat to rolling boil again, stirring constantly. Remove from heat and immediately skim off foam.

With ladle, fill one hot sterilized jelly glass at a time to within ½ inch of top. Immediately cover hot jelly with a ⅛-inch layer of hot paraffin. When paraffin is hard, check seal. Cover glasses with metal or paper lids and store in dark, dry place.

This makes 4 eight-ounce glasses.

THE HERB POT

It is good to keep an herb pot on your kitchen counter in which to put leftovers from minced sprigs of any fresh herb, which you have quickly dried in the oven as it cools after the roast or pie has been taken out. The little pot may be any small porcelain or pottery container that can be kept tightly closed. The combination of herbs inside will probably never be the same from day to day, for one day you may have more tarragon, or more parsley, or more thyme than other days. This pot can be kept going constantly as you snip more fresh herbs than you need for a particular salad or other dish. The herbs in this pot are very handy—during a thunderstorm, for instance, when you are loath to step into the garden for a snip of fresh herbs. From the herb pot you may take the pinches needed for the soft-boiled, poached, or coddled breakfast eggs. And if you have not snipped quite enough fresh herbs to give just the right touch to the casserole or soup or hamburger, another pinch from the herb pot fills in quickly. It is a splendid emergency supply.

HERB SUGARS

Herb sugars are made by layering white sugar and the fresh leaves of scented geraniums, lemon verbena, or mint, or fresh rose petals, each stored in its own tightly closed container. These delicately flavored sugars are used in whipped cream or cream toppings, frosting, meringues, and on fruit, eliminating the necessity to add vanilla or other flavorings to the sugar used in such foods.

HERB TEAS

No book about herbs would be complete without a mention of the pleasure provided by herb teas. They have been drunk for centuries for refreshment, for gentle stimulation, and for many kinds of ills and complaints and disabilities. They are steeped in the same way as are other teas, except that you should allow a few minutes longer to bring out the delicate flavors. Make them of either fresh or dried herbs, with or without the flowers. A cup of hot Orange Pekoe tea poured into a cup containing a single rose geranium leaf or several lemon verbena or mint leaves is delicious, too. Cream or milk are not served with herb

teas, according to tea epicures, for they cloud the delicate color and flavor and change the aroma. A drop or two of honey, however, smooths and blends and enhances a cup of herb tea. Bees and herbs, as well as honey and herbs, are "go-togethers."

The herbalists of old recommended teas made of peppermint, basil, or sage for relief from a touch of indigestion. They believed that angelica tea was good for coughs and colds; peppermint for headaches and nausea; rosemary for colds and "loss of memory" (rosemary for remembrance). If you wanted to live for a long time, they said, sage tea might help stretch your life expectancy (remember that old saying "He who eats sage in May will live for aye"?), and what is more believable, they suggested sage tea as a relief for headaches. For pure enjoyment, drink lemon balm, mint, lemon verbena, lemon thyme, sage, lavender, or sweet marjoram teas alone, or with Orange Pekoe tea, or mixed in a tea blend of your own, perhaps with a little spice.

HERB VINEGARS

Herb vinegars give a fresh taste to wintertime salads, and they add flavor to greens, summer or winter, if fresh herbs are not available.

You may use them in green salads, salad dressings, on coleslaw, in marinades, and in cooking wherever vinegar is one of the ingredients. You may also flavor summer drinks with burnet vinegar, for instance, which provides a cool fresh cucumber taste.

Herbs that make delicious vinegars are dill, tarragon, lovage, mint, basil (both green and purple), burnet, marjoram, and thyme. Garlic can be combined with herbs for a hearty flavor (but should be removed from the final bottle if herb vinegar is to be stored). It is possible to make herb vinegar of combinations of herbs, but as with *fines herbes*, you must take some care not to use too much of any one strong herb when mixing it with delicate herbs, or it will dominate the flavor of the finished vinegar.

RECIPE FOR HERB VINEGAR

1 cup white vinegar or white wine vinegar

One of the following:

   ¼ cup snipped fresh dill or ½ teaspoon dried dill weed

   ¼ cup snipped fresh chives

   ⅓ cup snipped fresh mint

   1 clove garlic, quartered (see above)

Shake ingredients in tightly covered jar. Refrigerate at least four days to blend flavors. Strain before using.

This recipe makes 1 cup of vinegar. For larger amounts, increase ingredients accordingly: for a quart of herb vinegar, multiply the amounts by four.

MARINADES

A marinade is a kind of sauce usually made of wine, wine vinegar, or fruit juice, spices, and herbs. Vegetables, fish, and meats are soaked in marinades to give them flavor and render them tender. They should be used in nonmetal containers because marinades in metal containers may take on a metallic flavor or corrode the vessel.

Marinades may be made of raw materials, or they may be cooked.

Most recipes that call for a marinade give the ingredients. There are endless combinations. French Dressing for salads is really a marinade, for it improves the flavor of the salads in which it is used. In this case, the marinade is eaten along with the greens. With meat marinades, you usually soak the meat and then drain it, often saving the marinade to flavor the sauce or gravy that is served with the meat. Fresh herbs are best for marinades if they are available, but dried herbs are satisfactory.

A *Bouquet Garni* of Kitchen Garden Suggestions and Recipes

EGGS WITH *FINES HERBES*

A favorite egg dish for lazy Sunday breakfasts, party breakfasts or brunch is baked or shirred eggs. For a new flair, add a teaspoon of butter and a pinch of *fines herbes* (or a teaspoon of herb butter) to each egg. Freshly grated Parmesan cheese may also be added with the herbs to the top of the eggs before cooking.

When friends drop in casually at lunch time, "put a new feather on an old hat" with herbs by adding a fresh herb garnish to Egg Salad Sandwiches, and serve them open-faced. This unexpected-guest luncheon special is easy and attractive, and it is a splendid way to try out different herbs for flavor.

Spread the egg salad on buttered bread (homemade if possible) then garnish with a nasturtium flower in the center (it is edible) surrounded by fresh leaves of *fines herbes* or any one minced chopped fresh herb you choose, such as tarragon, savory, marjoram, basil, dill, or fennel. You might serve the herbs instead at the table in a divided hors d'oeuvres plate, in each section of which is a different minced chopped fresh herb. Each guest may then choose his own herb topping.

You might also add to this attractive luncheon plate a few tomato slices, radishes, olives, and homemade pickles; or a head of Tom Thumb lettuce with Italian Dressing; and potato chips. Variations on the plate are limitless.

DILLED CUCUMBERS IN SOUR CREAM

Two inhabitants of the kitchen garden combine well in a dish that is excellent as an appetizer or served with cold roast meat, salmon, or chicken. Slice unpeeled fresh cucumbers and marinate the slices in French or Italian Dressing. Chill well and drain. Mix with chopped fresh dill leaves and sour cream and serve in a glass relish dish, or, for a first course, on a lettuce leaf.

EASY HORS D'OEUVRES, CANAPÉS, AND DIPS

You will have no problems making hors d'oeuvres, canapés, or a dip when callers arrive at the cocktail hour, if you have the kitchen garden at hand plus various kinds of cheese. Fresh crisp vegetables (little raw carrots, Tiny Tim tomatoes, radish roses) dipped in herbed mayonnaise are tempting. Thin mayonnaise with cream and add a touch of dry mustard and fresh minced herbs for this quick mixture. Or dip the vegetables into a mixture of cottage and cream cheese plus herbs, smoothed with cream.

To make canapés, spread the herbed mayonnaise or cheese mixtures on rounds of toast, Melba toast, fresh bread, or crackers; garnish with herbs and thin slices of peppers, cucumber, tomato, or radish. You may use many other foods in combination with cottage and cream cheese and herbs, such as tinned sardines, ham spread, shrimps or tuna, chopped ham, chicken or turkey, or crumbled bacon. Combine one, two, or several—mix them up and dress them up; the herbs furnish the flavor that puts all these spur-of-the-moment appetizers into the gourmet class.

One of the easiest, richest, and most popular hors d'oeuvres (an hors d'oeuvre is an appetizer that is not served on toast, bread, or crackers) is teaspoon-sized cheese balls rolled in minced fresh *fines herbes*, parsley, or other fresh herbs.

CHICKEN WITH TARRAGON

There are as many ways of preparing Chicken Tarragon (in France it is elegantly called *"Poulet a l'estragon"*) as there are chefs or cooks. An easy way to try it yourself is to add 1 tablespoon of minced fresh or fresh-frozen tarragon to the chicken of your favorite recipe, about 15 minutes before it is done. Try this in chicken that is fried, baked, oven-fried, in casserole, stewed, or in salad.

COLD MEAT AND SHELLFISH SALADS

Add minced lovage, parsley, chives, or tarragon leaves to your favorite chilled chicken, turkey, lobster, crabmeat, or shrimp salad. Serve the salad in a pretty crystal or china bowl with crisp lettuce leaves, and garnish with cucumber slices, radishes, chopped chives, and a parsley sprig or two.

MACÉDOINE OF VEGETABLES WITH SAUCE VINAIGRETTE

On a hot summer's night, a platter of cold cooked vegetables from the kitchen garden accompanied by a sauceboat of Sauce Vinaigrette is a combined salad and vegetable course. Then you can appreciate the beauty and glory of your garden, arrayed with artistry in lively colors and attractive shapes, garnished with tips of green herbs. Such a display is particularly good when served with a cooked whole fish, such as salmon (hot or cold), striped bass, bluefish, or pike; or with cold fried chicken, turkey, ham, or roast beef.

A combination of vegetables might be: fresh sliced tomatoes and cucumbers; cold cooked carrots, beets, asparagus (probably from the freezer), green beans, and peas; or really any choice that is available from garden or freezer. The vegetables should be just crisply done, not more, cooked in water with a chicken bouillon cube or two added, without salt. This can be done ahead of time and the vegetables cooled in the refrigerator, ready to enjoy by dinner time.

Since "macédoine" originally meant a kind of parsley, of course garnish the platter with fluffs of parsley; and you might also add hard-cooked eggs or small balls of Roquefort cheese rolled in finely minced parsley.

The Sauce Vinaigrette can also be made ahead of time and chilled; stir it well just before serving. Sauce Vinaigrette is useful for other foods, delicious ladled over cold seafoods in lettuce cups; on avocados or citrus fruit salads; on cold cooked spinach; and in mixed green salads.

In winter the platter is best served hot, with hot Vinaigrette Sauce. If you expect company, winter or summer, so much the better for showing off your kitchen garden dividends.

RECIPE FOR SAUCE VINAIGRETTE

1 cup olive or salad oil

⅓ cup lemon or lime juice or white wine vinegar

1 teaspoon honey

½ clove garlic (or to taste) or 1 clove shallot, finely minced

1 teaspoon salt

1 teaspoon dry mustard

¼ teaspoon freshly ground black pepper (or to taste)

1 to 2 tablespoons snipped *fines herbes* (parsley, chives, and chervil; or parsley, tarragon, and burnet)

1 tablespoon chopped capers

Measure all ingredients except *fines herbes* and capers into blender. Blend about 15 seconds. Pour into glass jar; stir in *fines herbes* and capers. Cover and refrigerate for at least 2 hours. Shake before serving.

This recipe makes about 1½ cups sauce.

KITCHEN GARDEN PICCALILLI

A tangy-sweet relish that combines many of the kitchen garden vegetables will have many uses during the year. The men in your family will especially appreciate it as an accompaniment to meats or game, and you may even use it to add zest to sandwiches and salad dressings.

RECIPE FOR NEW ENGLAND KITCHEN GARDEN PICCALILLI

4 pounds green tomatoes, chopped

4 pounds ripe tomatoes, chopped

4 medium onions, peeled and chopped

3 green peppers, chopped (seeds and membranes removed)

3 sweet red peppers, chopped (seeds and membranes removed)

2 large cucumbers (unpared), chopped

1 cup finely cut lovage leaves and stems, or 2 small bunches celery, chopped

⅔ cup salt

6 cups cider vinegar

2 pounds brown sugar (4½ cups, packed)

1 teaspoon dry mustard

1 teaspoon freshly ground black pepper

Place vegetables in large bowl. Sprinkle with salt and let stand for 8 to 12 hours.

Drain vegetables in a colander; gently stir with wooden spoon to remove as much liquid as possible. In large kettle mix vegetables, vinegar, sugar, mustard, and pepper. Heat just to boiling. Reduce heat and simmer for 1 to 1½ hours, stirring occasionally.

While mixture simmers, wash and sterilize 8 standard pint jars. With ladle, fill one hot sterilized jar at a time to within ¼ inch of top; wipe top and screw threads of jar with damp clean cloth and seal immediately as directed by manufacturer. Invert a few seconds. Place jars upright a few inches apart on several thicknesses of cloth away from draft. When cool, test seal, and store in cool dark place.

This makes 8 pints of piccalilli.

KITCHEN GARDEN GREEN SALADS

Early in the morning when the herbs and vegetables in the kitchen garden have had a night's cool rest, take a leisurely walk through the garden to plan a green salad for dinner. First, pick the lettuce and the cress, crisp and green. Add a few radishes. Snip off some leaves of chives or a bit of top onion. Then walk around the herbs, taking a snippet of this or that inviting one; perhaps one leaf of basil, a sprig of dill, a tip of marjoram or thyme. Each day choose a different combination. When the tomatoes ripen, oregano or basil will be especially good to garnish the glistening slices. When the cucumbers are ready, choose dill, chives, sage, or parsley.

Such a green salad ought to be dressed simply with oil and vinegar, salt, and freshly ground pepper. Perhaps you have a wooden salad bowl that is never used for anything else but salad, rubbed with garlic each time you use it. After use, wash it with clear cold water and rub it dry with paper towels. For company dinners, just to show off, use a fine mahogany bowl, or Grandmother's cut glass bowl. But the old maple bowl will be best, faintly redolent of garlic and herbs and smoothed with oil. "Never rub garlic on your wooden salad bowl," wrote one staunch herb lady, "you might want to use it for something else." But if you do not, do rub it with garlic.

If a more vigorous salad is desired, omit the herbs from the greens and add them to the dressing. Add other greens, perhaps escarole or endive, spinach or beet greens, perhaps some leaves from the field of mustard or dandelion. (A word to the wise here: it is best to know your field herbs before choosing them for eating, as not *every* green growing thing is appetizing or edible.) Dress them with a hearty Italian Dressing, made ahead of time and chilled before using.

RECIPE FOR ITALIAN DRESSING

1 cup olive or salad oil

¼ cup lemon juice

¼ cup white vinegar

1 teaspoon salt

1 teaspoon sugar

½ teaspoon dried oregano leaves (or 1 tablespoon fresh)

½ teaspoon dry mustard

½ teaspoon onion salt

½ teaspoon paprika

⅛ teaspoon dried thyme leaves (or ½ teaspoon fresh)

2 cloves garlic (or to taste), crushed

Shake all ingredients in tightly covered jar. Refrigerate at least 2 hours to blend flavors. Shake before serving. This makes 1½ cups of dressing.

A HAPPY ENDING

Every good meal should have a happy ending, and so should a book about kitchen gardens. Desserts incorporating herbs in some form have been served on American tables for more than three centuries. Tansy Pudding, for instance, a colonial favorite made from a useful strong-flavored herb, pleased our forefathers, but it may be strange to un-accustomed palates. Candied angelica garnishes cakes, cookies, and fruit compotes; fresh angelica adds flavor to fruit sauces and pies. Sweet basil, with its clovelike taste, may be chopped and added to fruit compotes. Bay leaf may be used in custards. Anise, caraway, coriander, fennel, sesame, cardamom, and poppy seeds give flavor and interest to cakes and cookies. Use lemon verbena and lemon balm leaves for garnish, or chop and add them to fruit sauces and compotes, cookies, and cakes. The various mints used for garnish may also be chopped and added to fruit dishes, jellies, dessert sauces, and puddings. The flavor of rosemary enhances jellies, pound cakes, and cookies.

A simple yet elegant dessert for family or company dinners will top the day and the dinner, with a touch of sweet herbs to add fragrance, flavor, and beauty. Such a dessert is Minted Fruits.

RECIPE FOR MINTED FRUITS

2 tablespoons sugar
¼ cup snipped fresh mint leaves
½ cup mint-flavored apple jelly
2 tablespoons water
3 cups assorted cut-up fresh fruits

Sprinkle sugar on mint leaves in small bowl; let stand 1 hour. Melt jelly in small saucepan over low heat. Remove from heat. Stir in mint-sugar mixture and water. Chill.

Arrange chilled fruits in dessert dishes; spoon syrup on each serving and garnish with a sprig of fresh mint. This makes 6 servings (¾ cup sauce).

Various fruits may be used, in combinations to your taste. Suggested are:

Sections of fresh, pared oranges and grapefruit;
Peeled, sliced banana;
Pared fresh, or canned, pineapple wedges or chunks;
Unpeeled, halved fresh apricots;
Peeled, sliced fresh peaches;
Fresh grapes, halved and seeded;
A variety of fresh berries such as halved strawberries, whole raspberries, blueberries;
A touch of grated fresh or dried coconut.

Si finis bonus est, totum bonum erit.
(If the end be well, all will be well.)

Glossary

ANNUAL: A plant that lives for only one season or year; plants that grow from seed, attain full growth, flower, and produce seed in a year or less, then die.

BIENNIAL: A plant that lasts for two years, usually producing its flowers and seed the second year, then dying. Some biennials may produce flowers the first year if sown early enough indoors. Examples: hollyhock, pansy, parsley, angelica.

BLANCH: In cookery, to immerse in boiling water to remove the skin, or to remove any bacteria that might cause spoilage.

In horticulture, to bleach (leeks, celery, etc.) by covering with earth or heavy paper collars so as to keep away light and improve the flavor, appearance, or tenderness.

BONSAI: Dwarfed and shaped trees, shrubs, or plants that are controlled by pruning and fertilizing.

BROADCAST: To scatter seeds by hand, in all directions.

COMPOST: A mixture of decomposed organic materials, such as vegetable refuse, manure, and leaves, for fertilizing and conditioning the soil.

CUTTING: In horticulture, a slip or shoot cut away from a plant for rooting to make a new plant.

DAMPING-OFF: A fungus disease or mildew that attacks seedlings, causing them to wither and die.

DRILL: A furrow in which seeds are planted.

FLAT: A shallow box or container to fill with soil for starting seeds.

FRIABLE: Easily crumbled, as of soil when it is crushed in the hand; a loamy texture of soil.

HARDEN OFF: To toughen young plants that have been started indoors, so as to accustom them to outdoor conditions, temperatures, and sunlight.

HILL: A small mound of soil heaped around plants; also a mound of soil in which plants are rooted; also ground-level planting places in which seeds are inserted, as "hills" of corn.

HUMUS: Organic part of the soil resulting from decay of leaves and other vegetable matter.

LAYERING: A method of propagating plants by bending a shoot, twig, or branch to the ground and covering it with earth until it has rooted.

LIME: A powder made from limestone that improves soil, reduces acidity, aids in decomposition of organic matter, and changes the chemical composition of the soil to help the growth of most plants. It should not be used on acid-loving plants such as azaleas or blueberries. It is best scattered over soil in winter or early spring and dug in before planting. It is not a fertilizer, it is a soil conditioner. The best for kitchen garden use is hydrated lime for clay soil, or ground limestone for sandy soils.

LOAM: A good soil composed of clay, sand, and organic matter (humus).

MANURE TEA: A liquid used for boosting growth of plants, made by putting manure (use a burlap bag for convenience in handling) into a container and adding water to a ratio of approximately 1 part of manure to 3 or 4 parts of water, depending on the strength wanted. If strong, the mixture must be diluted for use on seedlings.

MULCH: Leaves, straw, or other loose material spread on the ground around plants to prevent evaporation of water from the soil, weed growth, and frost-heaving of roots.

PERENNIAL: A plant that has a life cycle of more than two years.

ROOT CUTTING: A piece of root cut off a main root and used to propagate a new plant.

ROOT DIVISION: Dividing plants, including roots, into sections for the purpose of propagating new plants.

Seed Heads: Flower heads that have gone to seed, as dill.

Sets: Bulbs, twigs, or slips for planting.

Slips: Stems, twigs, etc., cut or broken from a plant, used for rooting or grafting new plants.

Snippings: Small pieces (of fresh herbs) cut or pinched off the ends of branches, in a culinary sense such pieces being used for seasoning foods as in *bouquets garnis* or *fines herbes* or for mincing and adding to foods for flavor or garnish.

Sods: Surface layers of earth containing grass plants with their matted roots.

Stem Cutting: A piece of stem cut from a plant for the purpose of rooting and propagating new plants.

Succession Planting: The practice of replacing an early crop, when harvested, with one that will occupy part or all of the space for the balance of the growing season.

Sweet Herbs: Herbs used for cookery.

Symbiosis: The living together of unlike (plant) species to the mutual benefit of each.

Thinning: Eliminating surplus seedlings to give the remaining plants necessary room to grow.

Tilth: A desirable crumbly condition of the land resulting from proper cultivation of the soil.

Trimming: Clipping or cutting, usually for the purpose of harvesting or to improve the appearance of a plant.

Tussie-Mussie: A tightly gathered fragrant bouquet of herbs and flowers meant to be carried in the hand, usually with a lacy paper frill around the outside.

Winter-Kill: Death of plants caused by varied weather conditions after the end of the growing season and before the spring growing season. May be caused by sudden or severe cold or frost that affects the plant roots and tissues; by winds that dry evergreen leaves (particularly) or other plant buds; by alternate freezing and thawing of the ground that tears the roots or heaves the plants out of the ground; or by other climatological factors. A heavy snow cover is a beneficial blanket that reduces the dangers of winter-kill, and a mulch of loose material such as evergreen branches or hay also prevents many winter injuries.

WOOD ASHES: From hardwoods such as oak, maple, or ash trees, ashes add valuable mineral elements such as potash, phosphoric acid, and calcium, when used on gardens. They are best applied to the soil in spring, scattered at the rate of 4 to 10 pounds per 100 square feet and raked or dug into the soil before planting. They may also be dug in lightly around plants to discourage slugs and cutworms. Wood ashes help neutralize acid soils. They quickly "leach out" or filter away with rainfall and can be used in any reasonable quantity without danger to plants.

Some Sources for
Seeds, Plants, and Garden Needs

NEW ENGLAND

Caprilands Herb Farm
Coventry, Connecticut 06238

Logee's Greenhouses
55 North Street
Danielson, Connecticut 06239

The Charles C. Hart Seed Company
Main and Hart Streets
Wethersfield, Connecticut 06109

Comstock, Ferre & Co.
263 Main Street
Wethersfield, Connecticut 06109

Merry Gardens
P.O. Box 595
Camden, Maine 04853

Greene Herb Gardens, Inc.
Greene, Rhode Island 02827

Putney Nursery, Inc.
Putney, Vermont 05346

EAST

Cottage Herb Farm Shop
311 State Street
Albany, New York 12210

Stokes Seeds, Inc.
Box 548, Main P.O.
Buffalo, New York 14240

Burnett Brothers, Inc.
92 Chambers Street
New York, New York 10007

The City Gardener
53 Irving Place
New York, New York 10003

The Tool Shed Herb Nursery
Turkey Hill Road, Salem Center
Purdy Station, New York 10578

Joseph Harris Company
Moreton Farm
Rochester, New York 14624

Carroll Gardens
444 East Main Street
P.O. Box 310
Westminster, Maryland 21157

W. Atlee Burpee Company
300 Park Avenue
Warminster, Pennsylvania 18974

The Herb Cottage
The Washington Cathedral
Mount St. Alban
Washington, D.C. 20016

SOUTH

The George W. Park Seed Co., Inc.
P.O. Box 31
Greenwood, South Carolina 29646

Hilltop Farm & Garden Center
Box 866
Cleveland, Texas 77327

MIDWEST

R. H. Shumway Seedsman
628 Cedar Street
Rockford, Illinois 61101

Indiana Botanic Gardens, Inc.
P.O. Box 5
Hammond, Indiana 46325

W. Atlee Burpee Company
P.O. Box B-2001
Clinton, Iowa 52732

Earl May Seed & Nursery Company
Shenandoah, Iowa 51601

Henry Field Seed & Nursery Co.
Shenandoah, Iowa 51602

Farmer Seed & Nursery Company
Faribault, Minnesota 55021

Sunnybrook Farms Nursery
9448 Mayfield Road
Chesterland, Ohio 44026

Spring Hill Nurseries
Tipp City, Ohio 45371

Gurney Seed & Nursery Company
Yankton, South Dakota 57078

WEST

Mail Box Seeds
2042 Encinal Avenue
Alameda, California 94501

Herb Products Company
11012 Magnolia Boulevard
North Hollywood, California 91601

W. Atlee Burpee Company
P.O. Box 748
Riverside, California 92502

Taylor's Garden
2649 Stingle Avenue
Rosemead, California 91770

Index